CW00894135

Jane Eyre

Open Guides to Literature

Series Editor: Graham Martin (Professor of Literature, The Open University)

Current titles

Walford Davies: Dylan Thomas
P. N. Furbank: Pound
Graham Holderness: *Women in Love*
Graham Holderness: *Wuthering Heights*
Jeannette King: *Jane Eyre*
Graham Martin: *Great Expectations*
Roderick Watson: MacDiarmid

Titles in preparation

Angus Calder: Byron
Roger Day: Larkin
Peter Faulkner: Yeats
Anthony Fothergill: *Heart of Darkness*
Brean Hammond: *Gulliver's Travels*
David Pirie: Shelley
Ron Tamplin: Heaney
Dennis Walder: Hughes
Ruth Whittaker: *Tristram Shandy*

JEANNETTE KING

Jane Eyre

Open University Press
Milton Keynes · Philadelphia

Open University Press
Open University Educational Enterprises Limited
12 Cofferidge Close
Stony Stratford
Milton Keynes MK11 1BY, England

and
242 Cherry Street
Philadelphia, PA 19106, USA

First Published 1986

British Library Cataloguing in Publication Data

King, Jeannette
Jane Eyre. – (Open guides to literature)
1. Brontë, Charlotte. Jane Eyre
I. Title
823′.8 PR4167.J5

ISBN 0 335 15094 2
ISBN 0 335 15085 3 Pbk.

Library of Congress Cataloging in Publication Data
Main entry under title:

King, Jeannette.
Jane Eyre.
(Open guides to literature)
Bibliography: p.
1. Brontë, Charlotte, 1816–1855. Jane Eyre.
I. Title. II. Series.
PR4167.J5K56 1986 823′.8 86-2455

ISBN 0 335 15094 2
ISBN 0 335 15085 3 (pbk.)

Text design by Clarke Williams
Phototypeset by Dobbie Typesetting Service, Plymouth, Devon
Printed in Great Britain by J. W. Arrowsmith Ltd, Bristol

To Daniel and Jane

Contents

Series Editor's Preface

The intention of this series is to provide short introductory books about major writers, texts, and literary concepts for students of courses in Higher Education which substantially or wholly involve the study of Literature.

The series adopts a pedagogic approach and style similar to that of Open University material for Literature courses. *Open Guides* aim to inculcate the reading 'skills' which many introductory books in the field tend, mistakenly, to assume that the reader already possesses. They are, in this sense, 'teacherly' texts, planned and written in a manner which will develop in the reader the confidence to undertake further independent study of the topic. They are 'open' in two senses. First, they offer a three-way tutorial exchange between the writer of the *Guide*, the text or texts in question, and the reader. They invite readers to join in an exploratory discussion of texts, concentrating on their key aspects and on the main problems which readers, coming to the texts for the first time, are likely to encounter. The flow of a *Guide* 'discourse' is established by putting questions for the reader to follow up in a tentative and searching spirit, guided by the writer's comments, but not dominated by an over-arching and single-mindedly-pursued argument or evaluation, which itself requires to be 'read'.

Guides are also 'open' in a second sense. They assume that literary texts are 'plural', that there is no end to interpretation, and that it is for the reader to undertake the pleasurable task of discovering meaning and value in such texts. *Guides* seek to provide, in compact form, such relevant biographical, historical and cultural information as bears upon the reading of the text, and they point the reader to a selection of the best available critical discussions of it. They are not in themselves concerned to propose, or to counter, particular readings of the texts, but rather to put *Guide* readers in a position to do that for themselves. Experienced travellers learn to dispense with guides, and so it should be for readers of this series.

Page references are to the World's Classics paperback edition of *Jane Eyre*, edited by Margaret Jack (Oxford University Press, 1980). This edition has the advantage of preserving the three-volume divisions of the original, and contains helpful notes on the many literary and Biblical allusions. However, if you have difficulty obtaining this edition, you could use the Penguin edition, edited by Q. D. Leavis (1966), which has an excellent Introduction. I have included chapter references for use with this or any other text, but you should note that these do not correspond with the chapter numbering of the World's Classics edition.

Graham Martin

Acknowledgements

The author and publisher wish to thank the following for their permission to reproduce copyright material:

Annette Tromly and the University of Wisconsin Press for extracts from *Charlotte Brontë: The Cover of the Mask*, 1982; Sandra Gilbert & Susan Gubar and Yale University Press for extracts from *The Madwoman in the Attic*, 1979; Helene Moglen and The University of Wisconsin Press for an extract from *Charlotte Brontë: The Self Conceived*, 1976; Farrar, Straus and Giroux Inc. for extracts from Roland Barthes, *S/Z*, translated by Richard Miller, 1974.

For their suggestions at the earliest stages of this guide, I would like to thank Wendy Craik and Robin Gilmour, of the University of Aberdeen. Pam Slaughter and Jeremy Tambling provided fresh ideas and encouragement when they were most needed and much appreciated. My main debt, however, is to Graham Martin, for his advice and criticism at every stage in the writing of this book.

1. Who is Jane Eyre?

The aim of this *Guide* is to familiarize you with the themes and methods of *Jane Eyre*. Much of the emphasis will be on close reading of the text, and I shall ask you to consider and analyse short passages for yourself before you go on to read my comments. Each of the first three chapters concentrates on distinct and manageable sections of the novel, so that you can feel confident both about analysing brief passages and about considering the place of that passage within the section as a whole. Chapter 4 requires you to consider again all those sections of the novel previously discussed, but this time from a broader perspective. The remaining chapters deal with the novel as a whole, raising issues of critical theory, and considering alternative interpretations of the text. Discussion of the most interesting recent criticism, as it relates to *Jane Eyre*, is contained in Chapter 7.

But before you go any further, you should read *Jane Eyre* right through, if you have not already done so. You can then re-read the relevant sections of the novel in conjunction with the *Guide*, making notes and carrying out the written exercises as indicated.

* * *

This chapter of the *Guide* deals primarily with the opening chapters of the novel (Chs 1 to 4), which are set at Gateshead. Even when you read the novel for the very first time, you will have approached it with certain expectations: because of its title, you will have been looking for answers to the question, 'Who *is* Jane Eyre?'. But novelists have many different ways of satisfying our curiosity. They may provide a complete and authoritative statement of the situation and character of the protagonist, as if it were a matter of undisputed fact. Or they can feed such information to us little by little, in the process of telling the story. Often, we are not given simple information, or direct judgments as to character, but are provided with pieces of evidence, clues, from which to draw our own conclusions. The novelist points us in the right direction by selecting details, constructing incidents, which will suggest particular aspects of situation or character. Instead, that is, of telling us, 'Mary was jealous of her sister', the novelist might write, 'Mary couldn't take her eyes off her sister's new dress'. Let's look at the way Charlotte Brontë introduces the character of Jane Eyre.

Please read Chapters 1 and 2 of *Jane Eyre*, making a note of everything you can establish first about the *situation* in which Jane finds herself. Then consider her *character* – what sort of person are we being presented with? And don't overlook the obvious.

DISCUSSION

The main character is a female child, as we gather from the fact that she is subjected to the 'chidings' of a nurse (p. 7). While clearly not a servant, she is nevertheless in a subordinate position, obliged to tolerate the young John Reed's abuse because she is an impoverished dependent. Jane has, we discover in Ch. 2, been in this situation since she was taken into her uncle's house as a 'parentless infant' (p. 16). Finally, her slight size gives her a sense of 'physical inferiority' (p. 7). These opening chapters emphasize Jane's vulnerability. A child, a female, an orphan, a pauper, and evidently unattractive, Jane is at every point disadvantaged.

When we consider her *character*, we have to take note of passages like these:

> I was glad of it: I never liked long walks, especially on chilly afternoons: dreadful to me was the coming home in the raw twilight, with nipped fingers and toes, and a heart saddened by the chidings of Bessie, the nurse, and humbled by the consciousness of my physical inferiority to Eliza, John, and Georgiana Reed (p. 7).

> 'She [Mrs Reed] regretted to be under the necessity of keeping me at a distance; but that until she heard from Bessie, and could discover by her own observation that I was endeavouring in good earnest to acquire a more sociable and child-like disposition, a more attractive and sprightly manner, – something lighter, franker, more natural as it were – she really must exclude me from privileges intended only for contented, happy little children.' (p. 7)

Thomas Bewick, *History of British Birds*, Vol. II, 1797.
'The fiend pinning down the thief's pack behind him, I passed over quickly: it was an object of terror.' (*Jane Eyre*, p. 9)

Thomas Bewick, *History of British Birds*, Vol. II, 1797.
'The words in these introductory pages connected themselves with the succeeding vignettes, and gave significance to the rock standing up alone in a sea of billow and spray . . .' (*Jane Eyre*, p. 8)

> With Bewick on my knee, I was then happy: happy at least in my way. (p. 9)

> Accustomed to John Reed's abuse, I never had an idea of replying to it; my care was how to endure the blow which would certainly follow the insult. (p. 10)

> The cut bled, the pain was sharp: my terror had passed its climax; other feelings succeeded. (p. 11)

The first quotation gives the reader an unexpected jolt, I think, following as it does the negative opening sentence of the novel, which one tends to read as a regret or complaint. Instead of the expected childish annoyance at having to stay indoors, Jane's response conveys an acute sense of both physical and emotional distress associated with such outings. Mrs Reed's comments in the second quotation appear to confirm that Jane is not like 'normal' children – she lacks a 'natural' 'child-like' disposition. But can we trust her judgment? Do we accept it as the mature judgment of an adult, putting a child's moods into a realistic perspective? Or do we judge it to be a totally inadequate response to Jane's evident unhappiness? Does the phrase 'contented, happy little children' reflect a reliable judgment? Or does it suggest a clichéd, sentimental view of children as a species which leads us to ask whether Mrs Reed is a good judge of the individual child?

You will have noticed also that Jane derives a muted kind of happiness from reading *Bewick's History of British Birds* (1797), a text illustrated with wood-cuts depicting its subjects in wild and desolate settings, dangerous to man. Her enjoyment of this gloomy work, and her imaginative interpretation of its contents, suggest that this lonely and unhappy child finds escape from reality in the world of the imagination. Her need for escape and the legitimacy of her unhappiness are established with the arrival of John Reed, while her instinctive acceptance of his abuse confirms she was telling the truth in describing herself, on the first page, as 'humbled'. It is only after she has suffered both pain and terror that this habitual passivity gives way to a violent sense of injustice.

In making your notes, you will have had to *evaluate* the different kinds of 'evidence' provided by the text, just as I have done. In considering the Red Room episode, for instance, what did you conclude from Jane's reactions there? What additional conclusions did you reach from the opinions other characters express about her behaviour?

DISCUSSION

I imagine you will have noted that the episode in the Red Room strongly conveys both Jane's helplessness and the rebelliousness and emotionalism which increase her suffering. Her strong and passionate sense of injustice combines with her vivid supernatural imaginings to create a condition of hysteria which ends in her fainting. What does this suggest to you about the nature of passionate feeling? Here is what Mark Kinkead-Weekes has to say about this often-discussed episode:

> There, red carpet, red curtains, red tablecloth, red hangings are set against the snowy white bed and chair, the bewildered face reflected in the mirror like a pale phantom. As the last daylight ebbs, so do the sustaining embers of Jane's rage. The life of the heart in this prison seems to present only a choice between frozen wintriness and red passion. . . . Yet the price of that kind of 'life' of the heart is underlined. 'A ridge of lighted heath, alive, glancing, devouring, would have been a good emblem of my mind when I accused and menaced Mrs Reed; the same ridge, black and blasted after the flames are dead, would have represented as meetly my subsequent condition.'[1]

As for the opinions that other characters hold of Jane, they are very unfavourable.

Bessie and Miss Abbot consider her 'less than a servant'. 'Under obligations' because of her poverty, she ought to make herself 'agreeable' to the Reeds (pp. 12–13). Finding her violence 'repulsive', Mrs Reed will only allow her out of the Red Room 'on condition of perfect submission and stillness' (p. 18). Why is Jane so unpopular? Surely because she won't conform to the behaviour considered appropriate to her dependent situation. Simply, she won't submit.

I hope you can see now why I've been so anxious to distinguish between *situation* and *character*. The Reed household find Jane intolerable because her character does not match, in their view, her situation. But it is just this perceived discrepancy which marks the originality of Charlotte Brontë's conception. Impoverished heroines, from Cinderella to Fanny Price, have traditionally achieved happiness through their patient acceptance of their lot, by which they demonstrate their moral superiority.

Does Jane's rebelliousness, as a punishable offence in the Reed household, merely add to her suffering? The following quotation suggests it has another, more positive aspect.

> Superstition* was with me at that moment; but it was not yet her hour for complete victory: my blood was still warm; the mood of the

revolted slave was still bracing me with its bitter vigour; I had to stem a rapid rush of retrospective thought before I quailed to the dismal present. (p. 14)

*'Irrational fear'

Jane's passionate sense of injustice temporarily keeps fear at bay. This potential source of strength is explored more fully in Chapter 4, which you should read now. Twice in this chapter, Jane's rebelliousness bursts out again. Do the two episodes differ in any significant way? What are the effects of these outbursts both on Mrs Reed and on Jane herself?

DISCUSSION

On the first of these occasions, Jane dares to criticize the Reeds: 'They are not fit to associate with me.' (p. 27.) She also asserts that Mrs Reed's behaviour is observed and condemned by her dead uncle and parents. She assumes, that is, the adult prerogative to judge her 'elders and betters'. On the second occasion, Jane is again offensively critical, but whereas her earlier outburst was involuntary – 'I had no control' (p. 27) – this time her protest is a more conscious decision: '*Speak* I must' (p. 36). Furthermore, she is protesting not only against Mrs Reed's lack of justice, but against her neglect of Jane's own specific needs: 'I cannot live so'. The strength of her anger, she implies, is directly proportionate to the strength of her need for love. Given love, she would have no need for hate. The responsibility for Jane's behaviour is thus laid firmly at Mrs Reed's door.

The first rebellion results only in 'bad feelings' (p. 28) for Jane, and prompt punishment from Mrs Reed, only momentarily 'troubled with a look like fear' (p. 27). But the second gives Jane 'the strangest sense of freedom, of triumph' (p. 37). As for Mrs Reed, she 'looked frightened', and you may have noticed that she addresses Jane in a 'tone in which a person might address an opponent of adult age' (p. 36). What does this suggest? What has she to fear from a friendless orphan?

What appears to terrify Mrs Reed is Jane's refusal to recognize her subordinate status. She attempts to conciliate Jane, to excuse her own conduct, above all to make Jane accept that, for a child, there are approved patterns of behaviour which cannot be transgressed. 'Return to the nursery – there's a dear' (p. 37) is surely an attempt to coax Jane back into the conventional, obedient role of the child, over whom Mrs Reed, as adult, can exert her usual authority.

Jane's triumph is short-lived compared with the poisonous feelings of remorse which follow (see p. 38). But this episode demonstrates the potential power of this otherwise totally vulnerable protagonist. Jane's ability not just to *feel*, but to *articulate*, a sense of injustice constitutes her only weapon against the world. In a child's hands this is, of course, a double-edged sword, resulting in many self-inflicted wounds, but its power is real.

Jane is a child for only a small proportion of the novel, and it is hardly surprising that an 'autobiographical' novel should begin in childhood. But is Jane's childhood presented simply as the prelude to her adult life? Or are there indications of cause and effect, linking the early and later years? Do you think that this question is so straightforward as to be hardly worth asking? We live in a society which assumes the importance of childhood as the stage of development in which the personality of the adult is largely determined. But historically, this is a recent view. As late as 1800, children were thought of as miniature adults. It was only under the impact of Romanticism, stemming in this respect from the influence of Rousseau, that our modern conception of childhood became dominant. Wordsworth's 'The Child is father of the Man' is probably the most familiar statement of this concept.[2] Once the psychology of the child was taken seriously, a form of fiction known as the *Bildungsroman* became increasingly popular, first in Germany in the 1770s, and later in the rest of Europe, in the 1840s. Translated as 'education novel', this term refers to novels tracing the development of the central character from childhood to maturity. Dickens's *Great Expectations* (1860–61) and George Eliot's *The Mill on the Floss* (1860) are among the most famous English examples.

But if during the Romantic period (c. 1780–1830), writers saw childhood as having an important formative function, they also conceived it as having important characteristics of its own. Many poems by, for example, Wordsworth and Coleridge, declare a belief in the innocence and natural goodness of the child, and so present childhood as a potent image of vulnerability. Exploring this subject in *The Image of Childhood*, Peter Coveney wrote of the Romantic poets, 'for them the child became the symbol of the greatest significance for the subjective investigation of the Self, and an expression of their romantic protest against the Experience of society'.[3] Coveney goes on to describe the 'flow of literary events' through which this Romantic vision transferred itself from poetry to prose:

> In this central transference towards prose, the flow carried within itself the characteristics of the romantic sensibility – the self-awareness, the

> heightened sense of individual personality, the social protest, and, too, the increased awareness of the child, as a vehicle for social commentary, as a symbol of innocence and the life of the imagination, as an expression also of nostalgia, insecurity, and one can just detect it, introspective self-pity.[4]

In what ways might Charlotte Brontë's presentation of Jane have been influenced by such ideas?

DISCUSSION

Charlotte Brontë presents Jane as an isolated figure. Without family or friends, she has no one with whom she can really share her thoughts and feelings. Even the occasionally friendly Bessie is limited both in understanding and sympathy. And Jane's character is, as we have seen, not one that endears her to others. Her situation and her character, then, incline her to lonely introspection, encouraging a preoccupation with her own feelings. But as well as inducing self-pity, this isolation from all those around her also puts her in a position from which to criticize her own small world. Although her own experience is severely limited, her reading has introduced her to a wider world, and to an awareness of moral issues which enables her to generalize from her own personal sufferings; the life of the imagination, therefore, fosters a sense of social injustice. The first-person narrative method provides the means by which this rich inner life can be fully expressed; the presence of the adult narrator, which we shall discuss in the following pages, enables that inner life to be explored from a more mature and analytical perspective. This dual emphasis on Jane's inner life, and on the challenge that the child presents to the adult world, seems to me to place the novel firmly within the important literary tradition discussed above.

Which brings us to the question: who is telling the story? Who is providing us with these initial impressions of the child Jane? And, of course, it is the adult Jane recounting the tale of her earlier life. So, what is the effect of this narrative method on the reader's relationship to the teller and the tale? What is the relationship between the child who is the subject of the tale, and the adult who tells it – who is herself, in a different sense, its real subject? Can we rely on the adult narrator to tell the whole truth of her childish situation? Or is the 'evidence' being doctored to give a specially favourable view? It is questions like these that have made the fictional autobiography, as a novelistic genre, vulnerable to the charge of being the 'fiction of special pleading'.

Here are two passages, the first from Chapter 2 of *Jane Eyre*, the second from Jane Austen's *Mansfield Park*. There are clear similarities between the situation of Austen's Fanny Price – another ten-year-old poor relation taken to live with rich relatives – and Jane. Like Jane, Fanny is oppressed by a sense of social, physical and intellectual inferiority, an inferiority stated even by the servants; she is afraid, as Jane is afraid, unhappy as Jane is.

> Daylight began to forsake the red-room; it was past four o'clock, and the beclouded afternoon was tending to drear twilight. I heard the rain still beating continuously on the staircase window, and the wind howling in the grove behind the hall; I grew by degrees cold as a stone, and then my courage sank. My habitual mood of humiliation, self-doubt, forlorn depression, fell damp on the embers of my decaying ire. All said I was wicked, and perhaps I might be so: what thought had I been but just conceiving of starving myself to death? That certainly was a crime: and was I fit to die? Or was the vault under the chancel of Gateshead church an inviting bourne? In such vault I had been told did Mr Reed lie buried; and led by this thought to recall his idea, I dwelt on it with gathering dread. (p. 16)

> Fanny, whether near or from her cousins, whether in the school-room, the drawing-room, or the shrubbery, was equally forlorn, finding something to fear in every person and place. She was disheartened by Lady Bertram's silence, awed by Sir Thomas's grave looks, and quite overcome by Mrs Norris's admonitions. Her elder cousins mortified her by reflections on her size, and abashed her by noticing her shyness; Miss Lee wondered at her ignorance, and the maid-servants sneered at her clothes; and when to these sorrows was added the idea of the brothers and sisters among whom she had always been important as play-fellow, instructress, and nurse, the despondence that sunk her little heart was severe . . . she crept about in constant terror of something or other; often retreating towards her own chamber to cry; and the little girl who was spoken of in the drawing-room when she left it at night, as seeming so desirably sensible of her peculiar good fortune, ended every day's sorrows by sobbing herself to sleep. (*Mansfield Park*, edited by Tony Tanner, Penguin, 1966, Ch. 2, p. 51.)

Is the reader as involved in Fanny's misery as in Jane's? Is Fanny's situation presented in such a way as to emphasize the child's misery and consequently the unfeeling behaviour of those around her? How do these two extracts compare with each other?

DISCUSSION

Although phrases like 'little heart' make an obvious appeal for sympathy for the child Fanny, and her distress is made clear, I don't think that we become as involved in Fanny's experience as we do in Jane Eyre's. The methods employed in each novel are so different as to create very different effects. The first passage dramatizes a single incident, whereas the second summarizes Fanny's experiences over a period. This kind of 'telling' tends to place the reader at a distance from the narrative, as opposed to the immediacy of the enactment of a particular incident, a 'showing'.[5] Equally important is the use of the first person. Jane's innermost thoughts and feelings reach the reader directly, so that we feel demands are being made on us to enter into that experience. In contrast, the use of the third person in the *Mansfield Park* extract enables the adults to be presented in their own right, not just from Fanny's point of view: indeed their view of *her* is juxtaposed with her own sense of her situation in the final sentence quoted. You can imagine how very different the Jane Austen passage would be if presented wholly from Fanny's point of view. But, of course, Jane Austen had her own way of shaping a novel, which rules out such a method.[6]

Does this mean that the Jane who experiences these events is the Jane who tells the story? Read to the end of the paragraph from which I have just quoted. Is the child Jane capable of making such an assessment of Mrs Reed?

DISCUSSION

These final sentences are clearly not consistent with Jane's later outbursts against Mrs Reed. Even if inconsistency is plausible for a child in such a situation, there is a change in the language which suggests that we are hearing the voice of a mature narrator, looking back with the advantages of hindsight and the understanding that comes only when the intensity of the immediate emotion has dissipated. Compare the emotive epithets in the earlier part of the passage – 'forsake', 'drear', 'howling', 'cold as a stone' – and the anxious rhetorical questions conveying doubt, with the final two sentences of the paragraph, written in the language of analysis and reason. Notice the parenthetical, 'I dare say', 'how could she' and 'it must have been', all conveying the desire to see reason, to see another point of view. Phrases like 'a strange child' and 'an uncongenial alien' are detached and dispassionate descriptions estranging the narrator from her own younger self, descriptions which deliberately adopt an external rather than internal perspective.

Try the following exercise for yourself. Read the description on p. 17 of Jane's fears that her uncle's spirit might appear before her. At what point does the adult narrator's understanding enter into and modify the child's perception, and what variation in style conveys this shift in perspective?

I have suggested that the reader is invited to enter into the young Jane's experience, but it is also true that the adult perspective is simultaneously present, imposing restraints on the reader's involvement. We are never allowed to be so involved in Jane's experience that we cannot also make rational judgements on her responses or grasp the wider moral issues involved. Moreover, Jane's early experiences are consequently placed within the context of the adult Jane's development. To put it at its crudest, we know that the child's anguish is not fatal: she lives to tell the tale. Moreover, it has been pointed out that these interventions by the adult narrator imply a structure of growth in the novel. They alert us to the fact that the Jane that tells is not the same as the Jane that suffers. Even before we can guess how or why she changes, the voice of the adult narrator makes us aware that she *has* changed.[7]

In studying p. 17, you will have noticed that, in this incident, the adult narrator's understanding casts doubt on the reliability of young Jane's perceptions. It is clear that Jane's imagination is working overtime under the stress of her misery and fear of being alone in the room in which her uncle died. Further evidence of this readiness to dramatize both herself and her situation can be found on p. 14, when she looks in the looking-glass and sees not herself, but a 'tiny phantom'. Again the adult narrator is there to remind us of the gap between imagination and reality: 'All looked colder and darker in that visionary hollow than in reality.' Because the child's emotionalism and imagination render her perceptions faulty at times, the presence of the adult narrator is crucial. Even this mature perception is subjective, of course, in that it represents the view of the one person who experienced those events now 'recollected in tranquillity', to use Wordsworth's phrase. But the 'showings' in the novel, dramatized events which usually include dialogue, provide a kind of control. They enable us to 'see' and 'hear' the evidence of the world exterior to Jane, including other people, for ourselves. We can test Jane's reliability against our own assessment of the evidence.

One particular feature of this narrative method is the occasional use of direct addresses to the reader. If you look ahead to Ch. 9, you will find the earliest example in the novel: asking herself whether her new friend Mary Wilson was not greatly inferior to Helen Burns, Jane replies, 'True, reader; and I knew and felt this' (p. 79). What is the effect of such an interpolation of the narrator's comment? Does it create a distance between the narrator and her subject? Or do the narrator and the subject tend to merge, particularly as the subject becomes a grown woman, rather than a child? Here are two comments on the issue:

(a) That most famous of apostrophes, 'Reader, I married him,' marks, among other things, a concise statement of the double orientation: the 'I' poised between 'reader' and 'him', between writing and experience. By reminding us so frequently of the narrative act, by calling us away from the recorded events to the reader/writer relation, Jane inevitably places us at one remove from those events.[8]

(b) These gratuitous addresses crop up . . . because Charlotte Brontë knows that her themes and characterizations run counter to conventional patterns of fiction, and she feels compelled occasionally to *assert* a community between the narrator and his (sic) presumable audience.[9]

Which of these views comes closest to describing your sense of the narrative? Are they incompatible?

DISCUSSION

Critic (b)'s argument rests on an assumption that our discussion of Jane's character has verified: Jane is not presented as a conventional little girl. The sentence just quoted from Ch. 9, where Jane answers an implied criticism, gives further support to this view. If these addresses 'assert a community' *only* between reader and narrator, this interpretation is, moreover, compatible with that of critic (a), allowing for a slight difference of emphasis. But this is the crux of the question. Most of these apostrophes invite the reader to share a confidence or feeling that Jane, for various reasons, is unable to express to any character in the novel (Ch. 37, p. 453, provides a good example). Do they then direct our attention to Jane's feelings *at the time*, inviting intimacy between reader and *narrated* Jane? Critic (a) suggests that the reader is invited to share only in the act of retrospection. Although the occasions which explicitly direct our attention to the narrative act are few – 'a gentle delineation' (Ch. 29, p. 349) and 'Hear an illustration' (Ch. 36, p. 429) are the most striking I have found – these interpolations do occur at moments of heightened emotion, recalling us from the emotional past to the present of the narrating at those points in the novel when we are most likely to become involved in Jane's feelings. Furthermore, they increase in frequency as the narrated Jane gets *older*, closer in time to the narrator, drawing the reader's attention to the *distinction* between the two Janes as they appear to be on the point of merging. They thus maintain the distance between the narrated Jane and the *reader*. In contrast, this increase in frequency is not so well accounted for by critic (b)'s theory, as the later parts of the novel tend to be *more* rather than less conventional: in the last two chapters dealing with Jane's marriage, for instance, we find as many as three apostrophes to the reader within two pages.

My own feeling is that the effect of these direct addresses is less clear-cut than either critic suggests; at times they direct our attention to the narrated Jane, at times to the narrator. Nevertheless, the very term 'reader' reminds us that we are involved in a 'literary' experience, so that I am inclined to agree with critic (a) that their overall effect is to focus attention on the *presentation* of Jane's experiences, even as we are invited to share in them.[10]

We have discussed so far the ways in which the character of Jane is established – through dramatization and narrative, through external views and internal. None of these methods gives a complete picture. The reader has to piece together the different kinds of information, implicit and explicit, retrieved from the text and evaluate them. In comparing these different elements which compose the structure of the text we must not underestimate the effect of the first-person narrative, which as we have seen 'privileges' Jane's view over that of any of the other characters. The autobiographical function of the narrator creates a relationship between the reader and the narrator which must affect the reader's conception of the narrated self.

From our study of these first four chapters of the novel, we have, then, established not only the most important aspects of Jane's character and situation, but the means by which they are conveyed. And we have established that the first-person narrative method has a vital function in determining our perception both of the child Jane and of the adult narrator. You could now try some exercises for yourself. Read Ch. 3, which we have not discussed, and make notes on the following questions.

(1) What do Jane's reactions to Mr Lloyd suggest about her relationship to the Reed household? What is the effect on the reader of the sentence beginning, 'I felt an inexpressible relief . . .' (p. 19)?
(2) Where, in this chapter, are you most conscious of the adult narrator, speaking in retrospect? Notice the contrast with the child's immediate responses, e.g. 'so cruel that I think I shall never forget it' (p. 23).
(3) What do you deduce from Jane's love of *Gulliver's Travels*? Is it consistent with her love of *Bewick*?
(4) Is Jane's appearance of any great importance? Does it affect the way she sees herself? Does it affect the way others see her? Does it affect her situation? (See p. 26.)

2. Characterization

In the first chapter of this *Guide* we considered Jane Eyre's presentation of herself; but as the narrator she also presents every other character in the novel. If this narrative method affects the way we perceive and relate to the narrator, it must equally affect the way we perceive those other characters. Let us begin by considering Jane's presentation of a newcomer to her life. This will enable us to observe her in the process of getting to know and judging another person, a process which the reader can be said to experience vicariously. We shall be able to consider the presentation of this process, and what effect Jane's point of view has on the 'knowledge' of others she acquires. We shall concentrate in this chapter on Chs 5 to 10 of the novel, but I want to begin by looking back to Ch. 4, to Jane's account of her first meeting with Mr Brocklehurst (pp. 31–5). What impression do you gain of his character, both from his physical appearance and from his speech and behaviour? And what words and sentences account for such an impression? What does Brocklehurst's anecdote about his little boy suggest about his religious views, particularly in relation to children?

DISCUSSION

Physical appearance: On p. 31 I underlined the following: 'Black pillar', 'sable-clad' ('sable', an archaic word for black), 'carved mask'. These phrases suggest to me a figure barely human, a totem pole rather than a person. Black has obvious associations with death, while the hardness suggested by 'pillar' is echoed by 'stony stranger' and made explicit in 'grim face'. Such language emphasizes his inhumanity: even the information that 'it was a man' (p. 32) is withheld from the reader for several lines.

The narrator explicitly acknowledges the distorting effect a child's perspective may have: 'he seemed to me a very tall gentleman; but then I was very little'. When face to face with him, Jane describes him in terms reminiscent of Red Riding Hood's on meeting the wolf/grandmother – 'what a great nose! and what a mouth! and what large prominent teeth'. Such language is clearly intended to convey the vivid impression Brocklehurst makes on this child, rather than an objective portrait.

Speech and behaviour: Brocklehurst, for his part, is equally interested in Jane's appearance: 'Her size is small: what is her age?' (p. 32). He appears to feel no reservation about commenting adversely on *her* size; it doesn't occur to him that she only appears small relative to *him*. His remarks are addressed to Mrs Reed; he makes no attempt to make the child feel at ease. When he does address Jane, it is in the nature of a catechism, a series of questions designed to elicit certain standard responses. Jane's use, not of the 'ready and orthodox' answers, but of the common-sense logic of childhood – 'I must keep in good health and not die' – meets only with further religious platitudes. Brocklehurst's dialogue with Jane suggests a complete unawareness on his part of the child's point of view, a total unawareness that *his* perspective may be partial too.

Brocklehurst's view of religious education seems designed to encourage hypocrisy and deceit – good behaviour for earthly reward or out of fear, rather than for the love of God or morality. He insists on the virtue of humility, yet his own daughter's comparison of her silk gowns with the dress of his schoolgirls demonstrates his lack of that consistency he is so eager to advocate. Such inconsistencies in his dialogue indicate a character more given to observing the behaviour of others than analysing his own. He singularly lacks, moreover, the Christian charity his school is said to represent.

In other parts of the novel, these external observations of character in action are supplemented by Jane's own judgments. There is no such explicit judgment here. There is also something missing from Jane's presentation of Brocklehurst that is a very important aspect of her presentation of *herself*. Can you see what this is? And does the absence of any explicit judgment mean this episode is presented *without* judgment?

DISCUSSION

There is no internal view of Brocklehurst, no representation of his thoughts and feelings. The use of the first-person narrator means that the only insight we can obtain into the inner lives of the other characters is limited to whatever intelligent speculation the narrator is capable of. In the case of a child narrator this can be a severe limitation. How serious a problem do you think this is? We never get the chance, for instance, to see whether the motives Brocklehurst articulates are genuinely felt. Would such knowledge affect our judgment of his behaviour, or alter the balance of sympathies? The absence of any such information puts all the emphasis on the workings of *Jane's* psyche. Every other characterization is subordinated to this.

As for the question of judgment, that is surely *implied* in the juxtaposition of Brocklehurst's unbending and insensitive approach to the child with the responses of the child herself, given full emphasis by the narrative method? The adult's failure even to attempt to bridge the wide gap between the child and himself marks him, not Jane, as the one guilty of a 'heart of stone'. Brocklehurst's speech and behaviour, that is, are presented in such a way as to validate Jane's childish impressions formed on the basis of his appearance. Or, to put it another way, the appearance of the 'stony stranger' clearly has symbolic significance.

Which brings us back to my suggestion that the reader has no insight into the inner lives of characters other than Jane – is this strictly true? We shouldn't forget that there are Jane's conversations with Helen Burns and others with whom she is intimate, which permit plausible self-revelation on their part. And there is this use of symbolic description. Please read carefully Chs 5 to 7. Compare the first description of Miss Temple (Ch. 5, pp. 47–8) with the description of her reactions to Brocklehurst's reprimand on her provision of extra food (Ch. 7, p. 64). What differences do you notice?

DISCUSSION

In the first passage I noticed two characteristics. The first was the provision of precise details intended to create a picture of a specific individual. 'Fine pencilling of long lashes', 'purple cloth', 'Spanish trimming': such phrases suggest the narrator is carefully observing and recording what she actually saw. Further expressions such as 'according to the fashion of those times', and 'the mode of the day', attempt to locate that individual in a specific historical period. Such details foster the illusion that the writer is describing someone who really existed. Secondly, I noticed the number of rather imprecise adjectives generally denoting approval – 'fair', 'shapely', 'fine', 'refined', 'stately' and 'clear'. None of these terms in themselves creates the kind of precise effect to which the first set of examples contributes. What they do, however, is to draw on the assumption that the reader and narrator are in general agreement as to what these terms imply, because they both inhabit the same world and share the same values. This, like the details mentioned above, is a common strategy of 'realist' fiction, since it implies that the fictional world of the novel belongs to the same order of reality as the world inhabited by the reader.

The second passage is more figurative than literal. The similes 'pale as marble' and 'as if it would have required a sculptor's chisel to open it', alert the reader to the possibility of figurative meaning in the rest of the passage. We are therefore ready to respond to a symbolic potentiality in the physical description. And then there are the names of certain characters. 'Miss Temple' suggests one reading for the phrase 'pale as marble'. But how do we reconcile the positive religious and spiritual qualities implicit in 'temple' with the 'coldness and fixity', the 'petrified severity' of the stone imagery? You will remember that Brocklehurst, too, is likened to a stone pillar, though black in contrast to Miss Temple's pallor. Are we to take this traditional opposition of black and white – evil and good – as an indication that Miss Temple has to harden herself in order to stand up to Mr Brocklehurst? Or is this recurrent imagery, linking the two characters, an indication of certain limitations on Miss Temple's part, a lack of flexibility which makes her a poor model for someone of Jane's temperament? I shall leave you to draw your own conclusions on this subject, which you can compare with my comments on imagery in Chapter 3 (on 'Language'), and on religion in Chapter 6 ('The Morality of the Novel'). I've just said that the first passage was typical of 'realist' fiction – fiction, that is, that pretends to give a direct account of real life.[1] But in recent years the very concept of 'realism' has come under increasing scrutiny and challenge, especially its implication that 'realist' novels 'reflect' the real world. What is this 'real world' being imitated? Are we being offered an *objective* representation of reality? Or is it just the world of the – usually middle-class – writer, or more precisely, his or her view of it? And how can that largely non-verbal reality be imitated by the purely verbal form of the novel? In concentrating attention on the language of realist fiction, rather than on the so-called 'reality' it depicts, recent criticism has required us to be more aware of the strategies of 'realism', which tended previously to be rather taken for granted.

We touched on one or two of these strategies in our discussion of the description of Miss Temple. A structuralist critic such as Jonathan Culler, for instance, looks at the distinction we have just considered between literal and symbolic description from a different angle: he suggests that the reader *interprets* the physical details in different ways. Using the term 'recuperation' to describe the process by which the reader incorporates any given detail into an overall pattern of significance, Culler distinguishes between 'empirical' and 'symbolic' recuperation.[2] 'Empirical' describes the process by which we look for cause and effect: if Jane dresses plainly, we might deduce this is either because of poverty or a puritanical element in her character. If she continues to do so when about to become the wealthy Mrs Rochester, we may assume it is for the latter reason. Where a cause and effect explanation is not possible, symbolic recuperation comes into play. We interpret the detail as a symbolic expression of character. We cannot extrapolate Rochester's character as causing, or having been caused by, his possession of 'jetty eyebrows', therefore we are alert to the possibility that this kind of detail *symbolizes* some aspect of his character.

Furthermore, structuralists have challenged the idea that the most 'realistic', 'lifelike' characters are those that are the most individualized. Realism in fact employs highly conventionalized methods to create the *illusion* of individuality. This illusion is generated by a collection of attributes taken from a common and familiar pool. According to Roland Barthes, one of the most influential of structuralist critics, characterization – like every other element in the realist text – operates through codes. One such code he termed the 'semic' code, drawing on '*seme*', a term used in linguistics to indicate any feature which distinguishes one lexical item from another. For instance, the words 'man' and 'woman' have certain semes in common ('human', 'concrete', 'organic' and 'animate'), but are differentiated by the semes 'male' and 'female'. The words 'man' and 'boy' have in common the semes 'concrete', 'organic', 'animate', 'human' and 'male', but are differentiated by 'adult' and 'child'. In literary criticism the term 'seme' refers to any item in the text which signifies a distinctive feature, whether it be an item of physical description or a psychological trait. This is Barthes's explanation of the process by which character is constructed:

> When identical semes traverse the same proper name several times and appear to settle upon it, a character is created. Thus the character is a product of combinations: the combination is relatively stable (denoted by the recurrence of the semes) and more or less complex (involving more or less congruent, more or less contradictory figures); this complexity determines the character's 'personality'.

> What gives the illusion that the sum is supplemented by a precious remainder (something like individuality . . .) is the Proper Name, the difference complemented by what is proper to it. The proper name enables the person to exist outside the semes, whose sum nonetheless constitutes it entirely.[3]

Character, then, is the sum of the semes – the sum of adjectives, verbs, attributes and actions attached to each specific name. Barthes uses the term 'seme' to emphasize that all these elements function as signs. We have already seen that physical descriptions in *Jane Eyre* often carry connotations – meanings over and above the literal. Barthes calls such a seme an 'index', because it 'points but does not tell'.[4]

But how is the reader able to grasp what the writer is pointing to with such phrases as 'dark skin', 'cold, composed grey eye', and 'chin large and prominent', all applied to Mrs Reed? These details or semes only generate a sense of character because they relate in turn to our cultural codes – cultural and psychological stereotypes. Readers are unlikely to assume from such details that Mrs Reed is an easy-going, warm-hearted woman, because our culture assumes some kind of correlation between character and facial characteristics. Furthermore, it has formalized that relationship into such clichés as appear time and again in fiction. Those grey eyes, for instance, so often have a 'cold glint' to them, perhaps because of the association with metals? And the strong chin is often used as a sign of determination or courage: thus, we speak of someone 'taking it on the chin', that is, courageously confronting some difficulty. Such clichés draw on the most basic oppositions in our language, oppositions which permeate our habits of thinking and writing. With reference to Mrs Reed, the relevant oppositions are light/dark, and warmth/cold, and such figurative language is endlessly used to describe character – 'light-hearted' as opposed to 'gloomy', 'warm-hearted' as opposed to 'cold'.

In reading, therefore, we construct character from these verbal clues and usually do so with such readiness that the 'character' grows and develops in our imagination far beyond the precise parameters given for that character in the text. Much recent criticism has discussed this aspect of the reader's response, looking at the ways in which the reader fills in the 'gaps' in the text so as to produce a whole out of so many disparate elements.[5] This emphasis on the way that character is constructed through language in the text means, I think, that we need to reconsider our use of the term 'description', which can be very misleading. If I were to ask you to describe a close friend, you would be able to do so with reasonable ease and with sufficient accuracy to enable me to accost this friend at the railway station without risking considerable embarrassment. Moreover, I would be able to check the accuracy or truthfulness of your description when I came face to face with its subject. But when we turn to literary description, we are dealing with a very different situation. What is it that the author can be said to be *describing*? And how can the reader assess the truthfulness or realism of the description when there is no original against which to measure it? You may have answered that the writer is describing a character conceived in the imagination. But this does not alter the fact that, for the reader, character only comes into existence through the process of reading. There is no 'original' for the reader, whatever there may have been for the writer. When we describe a character as 'true to life', therefore, we need to consider carefully *whose* life we mean. Yours? Mine? The writer's? Life in general – whatever that means? We shall have to return to this and other questions relating to realism in Chapter 4.

How is this process of fictional characterization related to the first-person narrative method of *Jane Eyre*? It will be clear by now that when Helen Burns tells Jane 'not to judge by appearances' (Chapter 6, p. 56), this conventional piece of wisdom may need to be challenged. For it is precisely through Jane's observations of appearances that the reader is given some insight into the inner life of other characters.

Moreover, a kind of scientific validity – in nineteenth-century terms – was given to this emphasis on appearance by phrenology, the 'science' of judging character from the shape of a person's skull.[6] If personality is expressed on the body in this way, then Jane can interpret and judge simply on the basis of what she sees. References to this conception are numerous. They range from brief comments on the size of a character's forehead or 'front', such as occurs in the first description of Miss Temple, to more explicit references to the theory. If you look ahead to Ch. 14, you will find an example of Jane explicitly interpreting Rochester's head in this way:

> He lifted up the sable waves of hair which lay horizontally over his brow, and showed a solid enough mass of intellectual organs; but an abrupt deficiency where the suave sign of benevolence should have risen. (p. 132)

But even in her early life, Jane interprets the faces of those around her in this way: Mr Lloyd the apothecary has 'a hard-featured yet good-natured looking face' (Ch. 3, p. 23), and Helen Burns has a 'large, mild, intelligent, and benign-looking forehead' (Ch. 8, p. 74). Such readings of character can be seen as characteristic of Jane's function as narrator. And the more difficult problems of interpretation she will encounter later, when she meets men like Rochester and Rivers, are prepared for by her early *literary* readings, which expose her to a world far wider than her actually very narrow one. But in the meantime, *she* is read by others: Helen, for instance, tells Jane, 'I read a sincere nature in your ardent eyes and on your clear front' (Ch. 8, p. 70). More seriously, those adults who control her life interpret the 'text' of Jane from a very different viewpoint, attempting to impose on her *their* judgments and prejudices. It has been suggested that the task of interpretation is made easier for Jane by the allusions the characters themselves provide, often quite consciously, such as Rochester's references to Milton's Satan-allusions which relate to the literary experiences which form so important a part of Jane's life.[7]

How far does this view of Jane as 'reader' help to explain the effect of the narrative method on the presentation of character? The implication is that there are *two* 'readers' – Jane and the 'real' reader, you or I. This emphasizes that everything with which we are presented has been first filtered through Jane's consciousness, and in the process interpreted and evaluated. That is, Jane narrates only what she has first 'read'. Our perception of the other characters in the novel is, therefore, not simply limited to what Jane sees, but coloured by what Jane feels. Because they are presented through Jane's consciousness, they are inevitably measured against her values. This is not to say that in every case she passes an explicit judgment, but that each character or experience is 'placed' within a system of values generated largely by imagery and patterns of contrast and comparison. I suggested, for instance, that there might be significance in the use of the same stone imagery for both Miss Temple and Mr Brocklehurst. Let's now look at the way Jane 'reads' the character of Helen Burns. We can start with their first meeting (Ch. 5, pp. 49–52); how appropriate is the view of Jane as 'reader' here? Then read Ch. 8. What images does Jane use in connection with Helen? Does her name have any symbolic value?

DISCUSSION

You will have noticed that Jane is explicitly engaged in an act of interpretation when she first meets Helen (p. 49). She is trying to connect the two 'texts' inscribed over one of the doors of Lowood – that is, trying to connect the reality of Lowood with the spiritual ideal of charity vaunted in the inscription. Helen herself is reading

Samuel Johnson's *Rasselas* (1759), but this very moral and philosophical piece of fiction has no appeal for Jane, who prefers fairies and genii. This literary allusion suggests both to Jane and the reader the kind of moral principle that Helen represents, an impression reinforced when Helen advises Jane to read the New Testament, and to learn to love her enemies.

Before we turn to the question of imagery, it is interesting to note that, at the end of Ch. 7, Jane draws attention to the subjectivity of any reading of character – while at the same time implying that hers is correct! Writing of Helen's untidiness, she comments, 'such spots are there on the disc of the clearest planet; and eyes like Miss Scatcherd's can only see those minute defects, and are blind to the full brightness of the orb' (p. 68). But this image of the bright planet is not itself really developed in relation to Helen, except in so far as it conveys the idea of a perfection which is not of this world. It is, I think, Helen's surname which provides the key to what little imagery is used in relation to this character. On the one hand 'Burns' conveys the idea of fire, suggesting the passion which is so strong in Jane, and its danger. On one occasion this interpretation is reinforced by imagery – when Helen and Jane take supper with Miss Temple, Helen is encouraged to talk freely beside a 'brilliant fire', where her powers 'kindled' and 'glowed' (p. 73). But 'burns' is also the Scots for 'streams' (Helen tells Jane her home is near the border with Scotland). This associates Helen with Rivers, the clergyman, whose coolly rational self-discipline is most like the side of Helen's nature which we usually see. The presence of these two conflicting meanings suggests that Helen is repressing a deeply passionate nature, a view borne out by the imagery of martyrdom which characterizes her otherwordliness, as it does Rivers's: when she smiles at Jane, undergoing public humiliation, 'it was as if a martyr, a hero, had passed a slave or victim'; her smile is 'like a reflection from the aspect of an angel' (Ch. 7, p. 68). And this imagery can't simply be dismissed as an example of *Jane*'s tendency to dramatize. The physical violence implied by martyrdom is reflected in Helen's own language, suggesting perhaps the violence she is doing to her own nature: 'if we were dying in *pain* and shame, if scorn *smote* us on all sides, and hatred *crushed* us, angels see our *tortures* . . .' (p. 70, my italics). One final point for your consideration: 'Burns' is also the name of Scotland's national poet. Could this be relevant here, do you think? We will come back to Helen's character in Chapter 5 of this *Guide*.

I want now to consider the role these other characters play in Jane's development. Some critics suggest that Jane learns by example from other characters she meets, most of whom belong to one specific phase of Jane's development, to one particular location of the novel, and do not themselves change. Where characters do appear in more than one stage of the novel, they carry with them their most salient traits. (Rochester is the one possible exception to this rule – see Chapter 4 *Realism or Romance?*.) Mrs Reed, for instance, re-appearing in the Thornfield section of the novel, is as unfeeling as ever. There is no death-bed repentance or change of heart. Jane, in contrast, is able to break her childish vow never to call her 'aunt' again. Her moral and emotional growth is enhanced by her aunt's lack of it. It has also been claimed that Jane initially postulates irrational causes for those things she cannot otherwise explain, whereas in later life she is more inclined to find rational explanations.[8]

Other critics, however, see the relationship between Jane and the other characters as being much closer than this, proposing that the latter are extensions of Jane's own psyche – indices of her changing emotional state – which shows, in itself, no development.[9] Helen Burns and Bertha Rochester, for instance, can be seen as extreme alternatives available to her. When Jane is sent to Lowood as punishment for her rebelliousness and anger, she is exposed to physical and emotional deprivation which make her long for acceptance and approval, and to learn how to deal with her own painful emotions. Helen appears to offer an example of complete self-discipline. At the other extreme, when Jane's feelings for Rochester threaten to overwhelm her moral sense, Bertha embodies, by implication, sexual passion run riot. Both of these alternatives are rejected, because they offer false solutions, as far as Jane is concerned, to the crises with which she is faced. In this view, there is no real development in Jane, simply a consolidation of her previously fragile position, as the decline of those around her symbolizes her release from these false alternatives. Further evidence that Jane develops no more than any other character has been located in the narrator's references to phrenology:

> The interesting implications of a serious use of the ideas of phrenology and physiognomy remain: character for Charlotte Brontë is ultimately static; it does not develop. Dormant elements may be brought out by changed circumstances, but the essentials of character are fixed and unchanging.[10]

Which of these variously opposing views of Jane's development do you find most convincing?

DISCUSSION

Supporting the view that the characters merely represent aspects of Jane herself are: Mrs Reed, Helen Burns, Bertha Mason and St John Rivers, all of whom die – that is, they vanish from the novel, after fulfilling their role in Jane's life. Rochester survives after the option he represents has been rejected, but he is accepted by Jane only after he has, through trial and error, moved towards Jane's position. But has Jane 'survived' simply because she resisted these alternatives, these challenges to her own view of herself? Or, because she, like Rochester, has changed, and learned to reconcile the conflicting inner impulses these characters represent? The view that character in *Jane Eyre* is static seems a logical conclusion to draw from the principles of phrenology. But does this make sense of the way the novel itself works? What about Jane herself? And Rochester? On this reading, the changes that appear to have taken place in Rochester at the end of the novel simply indicate his reversion to the good man that he claims nature intended him to be, now that the adverse circumstances that distorted his nature are removed. But aren't the changes in him matched by changes in Jane, resulting in a complete reversal of roles? (See Chapter 4 of this *Guide*).

You won't be able to answer all these questions until you reach the end of the novel, but my own view is that Jane does change, as one would expect in a *Bildungsroman*. And the clearest evidence for this is provided by the voice of the narrator – more mature, more rational, less egotistical, than her younger self.

Finally, here are some exercises to do for yourself. Below are examples of physical description. Using the approaches outlined in this chapter, make notes indicating whether you think they are symbolic or conventional. (You can compare your comments with the discussion of imagery in Chapter 3 below, pp. 26–31.)

Rochester: In her first description Jane notes the following: 'breadth of chest', 'dark face', 'stern features and a heavy brow' (Ch. 12, p. 114). Notice the emphatic reiteration of these and other features generally characterized in the phrase 'dark, strong, and stern' (p. 117): 'broad and jetty eyebrows', 'decisive nose', 'grim mouth', and eyes 'dark, irate and piercing' (Ch. 13, pp. 121–2). How does the associated imagery contribute to the effect? Consider, for example, 'His whole face was colourless rock: his eye was both spark and flint.' (Ch. 26, p. 292).

Bertha: 'the lips were swelled and dark; the brow furrowed; the black eyebrows wildly raised over the blood-shot eyes' (Ch. 25, p. 286).

St John Rivers:

> his face riveted the eye: it was like a Greek face, very pure in outline; quite a straight, classic nose; quite an Athenian mouth and chin . . . harmonious. His eyes were large and blue, with brown lashes; his high forehead, colourless as ivory, was partially streaked over by careless locks of fair hair . . . there was something about his nostril, his mouth, his brow, which, to my perceptions, indicated elements within either restless, or hard, or eager. (Ch. 29, p. 349)

According to phrenological theory, harmonious features imply simplicity of character, in contrast to the rich complexity implied by irregular features. Notice the imagery most frequently used in relation to Rivers's appearance is stone imagery – for example, 'like chiselled marble' (Ch. 33, p. 382). Which other characters does this relate him to?

* * *

In this chapter, we have seen how the methods of characterization in *Jane Eyre* are intimately connected with the first-person method of narration – Jane the narrator *presents* every character and therefore affects our perception of that character. We have also discussed the importance of *imagery* in conveying character, and it is to the wider uses and effects of imagery that we shall now turn.

3. Language

So far we have talked about 'characterization' and 'first-person narrator', using familiar critical terms. But in each case what we have *really* been discussing is the *language* of the novel, the words used to convey 'character' etc. The terms of novel-criticism, whether 'character', 'plot' or 'theme', are convenient labels for the cumulative *effect* of certain groups of words: for instance, as we discovered in our discussion of character 'semes' (p. 19), we describe as 'Jane Eyre' the total effect of every detail of appearance and behaviour which is attributed to that proper name. This language demands close attention because its precise effects depend upon the particular words used. I'm sure you'll agree that whenever we have tried to summarise or paraphrase any extract or group of extracts, the result has always been a reduction of the original meaning. We shall begin by discussing the novel's imagery, the most familiar aspect of literary language. But we also need to be alert to its other aspects, particularly to those distinctive features which constitute a writer's 'style', if we are to understand more precisely how *Jane Eyre* achieves its effects. Although I shall be using examples taken from Chs 11 to 27, the points raised apply to the whole text.

In the last chapter of this *Guide* we saw that the first-person narrative method provides a central point of reference from which every character is evaluated. Here, let us consider the role of the novel's imagery as a system of values within which that evaluation can take place.

We can begin by comparing the imagery used by Jane, as narrator, with that used by Rochester. When he disguises himself as a gypsy, he 'reads' Jane as she usually 'reads' others. Please read Ch. 19 (pp. 198–207) carefully. What is Rochester's 'reading' of Jane? What imagery does he employ in relation to her? What imagery does the narrator herself use?

DISCUSSION

Rochester's reading follows the same phrenological principles Jane herself employs:

> The forehead declares, 'Reason sits firm and holds the reins, and she will not let the feelings burst away and hurry her to wild chasms. The passions may rage furiously, like true heathens, as they are; and the desires may imagine all sorts of vain things: but judgment shall still have the last word in every argument, and the casting vote in every decision. Strong wind, earthquake-shock, and fire may pass by: but I shall follow the guiding of that still small voice which interprets the dictates of conscience.' (p. 203)

Rochester sees in Jane a conflict between passion and reason, or conscience. Earlier in this passage he reads these passions from the flame that 'flickers in the eye'. This association of fire and passion is, of course, traditional. It is also crucial to our interpretation and evaluation of character in the novel, and to its thematic structure.

The 'gypsy' accuses Jane of being 'cold' because she is alone: 'no contact strikes the fire from you that is in you' (p. 199). Rochester, passion's advocate, is accusing Jane of repressing her deepest feelings. But Jane's narrative itself reinforces these associations. The 'gypsy' is described as wearing a red cloak, red being traditionally the colour of passion, as well as the colour of fire (see also the Red Room). Jane notes that the crone '*stirred* the fire', a further revealing detail surely? Indeed Jane finally asks, 'Don't keep me long; the fire scorches me.'

Now please read Jane's account of her visit to Mrs Reed (Ch. 21, pp. 232–43). What pattern of imagery do you notice there?

DISCUSSION

The one I notice relates to Mrs Reed who continues as 'icily' and 'stony' towards Jane as ever, but tries later to explain to Jane her shock at her niece breaking out 'all fire and violence'. Mrs Reed's 'ice-cold and clammy hand', 'her eye of flint', and 'cold lid' (p. 242) are all consistent with a corpse or the form of someone fast approaching death, but they also establish a clear contrast of character and values between herself and Jane.

But it would be wrong to suggest that such images establish a simple value-contrast between good characters of 'fire' and bad characters of 'ice'. You may have noticed that the terms 'flint' and 'stony', here applied to Mrs Reed, are used in respect of Rochester in the example I asked you to consider at the end of the last chapter. Neither is there any suggestion that either passion or cool reason is in itself totally desirable or undesirable. Fire warms, but can also burn; ice freezes, but can also soothe a fever. You might like to consider for yourself, for instance, the symbolic implications and suggested patterns of similarity and contrast in these names: Burns, Rochester and Rivers.

To explore this further, it will be helpful to turn to David Lodge's analysis, 'Fire and Eyre: Charlotte Brontë's War of Earthly Elements'.[1] Lodge argues that Charlotte Brontë uses a system of 'objective correlatives',[2] operating at both the literal and metaphorical level, to unite the very varied components of the novel. Central to this system are the elements – earth, water, air and fire. The meanings of her references to fire are, therefore, defined by their position within this system of opposing forces. That is, while the love between Jane and Rochester is expressed in fire imagery, images of earth and water are used in relation to those things that threaten it, whether it be separation or St John Rivers. The ambivalence that these images nevertheless possess is made particularly clear by Lodge's comments on the volcano image, used, for example, in Chs 20 and 24 (pp. 218 and 269).

> The volcanic image is extraordinarily effective in conveying the awe that colours Jane's relationship with Rochester even after fear has been overcome by love: the sense of the danger as well as the exhilaration of exploring hidden, perhaps forbidden, daemonic, subterranean depths of the life of passion. (p. 133)

David Lodge concludes that extremes of heat and cold are potentially fatal to Jane, both literally and figuratively. You will recall that in the first chapter of this *Guide* we glanced at the *Bildungsroman*-aspect of *Jane Eyre*: such novels inevitably raise the question of how far the experience of the child determines the character of the adult. Does Lodge's analysis help us answer the question for Jane?

My own view is that Jane's fear of these extremes can clearly be traced back to her experiences of overwhelming passion in the Red Room, and to the chill, emotionally repressive worlds of both Gateshead and Lowood. Her development, therefore, involves a compromise between conflicting elements in herself – the opposing demands of passion and reason. But her horror of being consumed by fire or drowned by flood is also a metaphorical expression of her fear of those threats to her integrity which come from such different quarters as Rochester and Rivers. These external forces threaten the delicate internal balance she attempts to achieve.

But it is not just people in this novel that are threatened by fire. When Jane agrees to marry Rochester, the horse-chestnut tree in the orchard is struck by lightning and split in half, symbolizing not only the separation to come, but the destructive power of passion. Thornfield itself is destroyed by fire – a fire started by Bertha Rochester, in whom passion has run to the point of madness. People and places are presented within the same figurative patterns, relating internal and external reality. That is, the narrator conceives of them all within the same terms of reference. Read Jane's first description of Thornfield (Ch. 11, pp. 94–109). Look closely at her description of the stairs, the gallery, and her own room, and then at her description of the drawing-room, and the upper storeys. What imagery does she use? Are there any striking contrasts? Are there any figurative links between people and places?

DISCUSSION

After leaving the cosiness of the housekeeper's room, Jane is intimidated by a sense of size and loneliness: words like 'high', 'space', 'wide' and 'long' reiterate the contrast with her own reassuringly small room. She likens the house to a church, 'vault-like', 'chill' and 'dark', rather than a home. Its exterior is 'picturesque', but again lonely in its surroundings. The darkness of Thornfield relates the house to its owner, and its loneliness to his self-imposed exile. You can compare this chill picture with Jane's description of Thornfield after Rochester's arrival (Ch. 13, p. 119).

The drawing-room at first excites Jane's imagination as a 'fairy place', linking it with her first meeting with Rochester. You will have noticed the crimson and white colour scheme, 'the general blending of snow and fire' (p. 105). Here the extremes of Jane's character and experience will be brought sharply into focus. The third storey rooms are 'dark and low', with furnishings so antique as to give them 'the aspect of a home of the past: a shrine of memory' (p. 107). Here even the prosaic Mrs Fairfax thinks of ghosts. Jane's comparison with 'a corridor in some Bluebeard's castle' paves the way for her first hearing of Grace Poole's laugh.[3]

These spatial images evolve from the physical world which is both external to Jane and yet part of her inner life in so far as we only see that external world through the filter of her consciousness. That filter can be seen most explicitly and imaginatively in operation in Jane's paintings, where the same continuity of imagery persists into these imagined landscapes. These paintings are, in fact, the most direct revelation of Jane's inner life, free from the censorship of conscience or rationalization. Read her description of them in Ch. 13 (pp. 126–7). They are intended, I think, as pointers to states of mind too complex for rational explanation. But it is worth comparing them with Jane's description of *Bewick's History of British Birds* (Ch. 1, p. 8). What aspects of Jane's paintings have their origin in Bewick? What elements has she added from her own imagination and experience?

DISCUSSION

The first painting depicts a female form drowned in a billowing sea. The second also portrays a female figure, personifying the Evening

Star, and characterized by 'dark and wild' eyes, touches of moonlight and vapour. The third represents Death, as figured in Milton's *Paradise Lost*. The image of an iceberg surrounded by a 'ring of white flame' reminds the reader that ice too can 'burn'. 'Black drapery', 'sable veil', the brow 'white as bone', and the 'white flame' belong to the same image patterns noted previously. Apart from the imagery, the most striking element Jane has brought to the watery and icy landscapes of Bewick is the female form, both as victim and as figure of light, piercing the darkness.

This is what Mark Kinkead-Weekes has to say about the paintings:

> The pictures show us that Jane's inner landscape is bleak and much concerned with death, the heart frozen or submerged – but the points of light, precious, definitive, spiritualized, make it plain that a life of the heart is asserted against its winter. The pictures refer back to the icy winter at Gateshead and the little girl in the window-seat looking at *Bewick's Birds*. They also refer forward to the terrible inner flood that will sweep through her after the travesty of her wedding-day; to the icy death of hope but also the unearthly light of her dream and to the barren life in the wilderness from which she will eventually be recalled by the revelation of her woman's shape, and by that miraculous voice calling her name and manifesting her true identity.[4]

This analysis suggests that the paintings are prophetic in respect of Jane's inner life, as well as retrospective. You can assess the validity of this view for yourself by reading not only the end of Volume II (Ch. 26), which Mark Kinkead-Weekes refers to, but the end of Volume I (Ch. 15). In both these episodes the deep-rooted psychic fears and experiences expressed in the first painting are brought to the surface. The image of the flood represents Jane's dread of the annihilation of her self, whether by passion or despair.

I suggested at the beginning of this chapter that the imagery provides a system of values in whose terms evaluation of the characters takes place. We have concentrated so far on the Thornfield section of the novel, but the dominant 'elements' image-pattern is equally relevant throughout the novel. If we consider, for instance, St John Rivers's attempt to persuade Jane to become a missionary (Ch. 34, pp. 393–415), the images used to describe his effect upon Jane are predominantly those images of ice which represent the opposite pole to the fire imagery: 'his reserve was again frozen over, and my frankness was congealed beneath it' (p. 400); 'I fell under a freezing spell' (p. 402). In Chs 31 and 32 (pp. 363–76) however, fire images are used twice in relation to Rivers, the first one describing the effect of the beautiful Rosamond Oliver (see p. 369). You can find the other for yourself by reading p. 372. What does it suggest about Rivers's spiritual vocation? If you read Ch. 35, you will find further examples where Rivers is described in terms of ice imagery, and the related images of stone and marble. Can you remember other characters conceived in these terms? You can refer back to the second chapter of this *Guide* for some suggestions.

This same image-pattern based on the elements can also be used to evaluate the different locations in which the events of the novel take place, pointing to those situations which represent security or threat to Jane's sense of self. You can carry out this 'evaluation' for yourself: which locations represent warmth and security, for instance, and which represent cold?[5]

There is one more secondary, but important, image-pattern to consider. Developing out of the youthful Jane's love of fairy-tales is a repeated use of 'fairy' or 'witch' images. Rochester repeatedly refers to Jane as a witch (see e.g. Ch. 25, p. 283, and Ch. 15, p. 150) or a fairy (see e.g. Ch. 13, p. 123). Both he and Jane depict their first meeting in terms of a fairy tale, and you might like to consider the implications of Rochester's whimsical narrative in Ch. 24 (pp. 269–70). We will discuss this question in the next chapter, but in the meantime you might like to ask yourself: does the 'fairy' imagery represent something of value to Jane? Or does it represent a danger?

One final point: whose imagery have we been discussing? The answer may seem to be too obvious to need stating. Every word in the text is Charlotte Brontë's. And like Shakespeare, she sometimes puts into the mouths of her characters imagery which has significance for the reader, rather than the speaker: Jane, that is, is not always fully *conscious* of the implications of the images she uses. But in autobiographical fiction, where the language is supposedly that of the narrator, the novel's imagery is an important indicator of the *narrator*'s internal conflicts and values – conscious and unconscious. If this is what it tells us about the narrator, what does it tell us about the narrative? What questions does it raise about Jane's *representation* of her earlier life?

The point has been made that any autobiographical narrator not only chooses what material to include in his or her narrative, but in what form to present it. Jane, for example, uses metaphors of heat and cold, drawn from her early experiences, to 'arrange' those and later experiences. The narrator presents her material according to a certain pattern.[6] If Jane exercises this kind of narrative control, it raises the possibility that this shaping element distorts the 'facts' of Jane's life, a possibility which you should bear in mind when we approach the question of 'realism' in Chapter 4 of this *Guide*.

So far I have focused almost exclusively on the novel's figurative language, with some reference to the descriptive vocabulary. I have done so because imagery has such obvious importance in terms of the novel's themes and structure (see below, Chapter 5). This is confirmed by the amount of critical attention it has received. Moreover, it is this aspect of language that has traditionally received most attention in literary criticism. But there is more to the language of a novel than its imagery, and recent developments in linguistics have helped to clarify this. Modern linguistics analyses the rules and the structures which enable the individual words or lexical items to have meaning. Where traditional literary criticism has concentrated on the semantic aspects of the language of the text – the meaning of the different lexical items – criticism from a linguistic perspective has suggested that the grammatical structures most regularly used by a writer are equally worth studying. Such a view is based on the concept of transformational grammar introduced by Noam Chomsky, who differentiated between the 'surface structure' of the text – the actual words used – and the 'deep structure', its meaning. This 'meaning' remains the same whatever transformations are performed on the surface structure. For instance, 'The man greatly liked the book' – a surface structure using the active form of the verb 'like', with 'man' as subject – can be transformed into the passive form, 'The book was greatly liked by the man', with 'book' as subject, without changing the fundamental meaning or 'deep structure'. The sentence can similarly be 'nominalized' into 'His liking for the book was great', the verb 'liked' being changed for the noun 'liking'. These changes nevertheless produce different shades of meaning and emphasis, which to some critics would suggest that the different surface structures cannot 'mean' precisely the same. An author's preference for some transformations rather than others can therefore be as significant in determining what we think of as an author's individual style as choice of vocabulary and figure.[7]

One of the attractions of linguistics for the literature student is, I think, its 'scientific' quality: it provides a terminology and explanations for language features which can help us define more precisely the source of our impressions and subjective responses. Linguistics can provide tools which help the reader to identify the characteristics of any particular use of language, literary or non-literary. But if these tools are not used carefully, the result can be simply reductive, simply descriptive, so that one is left asking, 'So what?' Linguistic analyses of style can sometimes make for very tedious reading, particularly for the non-specialist, although the conclusions reached can nevertheless provide valuable insight for the literature student.

Bearing these reservations in mind, then, I would like now to look at a passage from *Jane Eyre* from both a traditional and linguistic point of view. Read the following extract. What striking features of the language do you notice? What images are used? Does it contain any distinctive vocabulary? Are there any examples of unusual or striking syntax?

> My pulse stopped: my heart stood still; my stretched arm was paralysed. The cry died, and was not renewed. Indeed, whatever being uttered that fearful shriek could not soon repeat it: *not the widest-winged condor on the Andes could*, twice in succession, send out such a yell from the cloud shrouding his eyry. The thing delivering such utterance must rest ere it could repeat the effort.
>
> It came out of the third story; for it passed overhead. And overhead – yes, in the room just above my chamber-ceiling I now heard a struggle: *a deadly one it seemed* from the noise; and a half smothered voice shouted:—
>
> 'Help! help! help;' three times rapidly.
>
> 'Will no one come?' it cried; and then while the staggering and stamping went on wildly, I distinguished through plank and plaster:—
>
> 'Rochester! Rochester! For God's sake, come!' (Ch. 20, p. 208; my italics)

DISCUSSION

A traditional analysis might begin by considering the imagery in the passage. You will probably have commented on the appropriateness of the condor image to the inhabitant of the third storey: this threat from above is a wild, predatory creature, possessed of powers far beyond those of ordinary men and women, and belonging to an alien and hostile world. You may also have looked for links with other parts of the novel through the image of the icy mountain and other bird images. The use of highly emotive adjectives and adverbs – 'fearful', 'deadly', and 'wildly' – contributes to the sense of intense feeling and drama in the narrative. Other features you may have noticed include the three brief clauses beginning the passage, each one slightly longer than that which precedes it, which give the passage such a dramatic opening; and the rather archaic use of 'ere' for 'before'.

Without suggesting that there is no overlap between 'traditional' and linguistic approaches to textual criticism, I think nevertheless that the latter would focus greater attention on the structures used here. What, for instance, did you notice about the syntax of the phrases in italics, remembering the usual 'subject, verb, object' word order of English sentences? You will have noticed that both depart from this order, the first beginning with 'not', the second reversing the expected 'it seemed a deadly one'. The term for this device is 'inversion'.

Now read this short extract taken at random from Tennyson's narrative poem, *The Princess*, also published in 1847.

> Strange was the sight and smacking of the time;
> And long we gazed, but satiated at length
> Came to the ruins. High-arch'd and ivy-claspt,
> Of finest Gothic lighter than a fire,
> Thro' one wide chasm of time and frost they gave
> The park, the crowd, the house; but all within
> The sward was trim as any garden lawn. (Prologue)

I have underlined the first two inversions, but if I had not drawn your attention to this linguistic term, I wonder whether you would have noticed them? We are so accustomed to the idea that poetry continually departs from normal word order, so as to adapt to the requirements of the verse form, that we are not surprised by it. It is, in fact, the 'norm' for traditional verse forms. What, on the other hand, is its effect in prose?

Most prose focuses attention on what is said, rather than the manner of saying it; it aims at a kind of transparency. The effect of repeated deviations from the expected norm is, however, to draw attention to the language in a manner more characteristic of poetry. Charlotte Brontë's prose shows many such 'poetic' effects, and notably a pattern of inversions so much greater than that found in other novelists of the period that it constitutes a distinctive feature of her style.[8]

Attention has also been drawn to the frequency of 'paratactic' constructions in this novelist's prose – that is, sequences of clauses which are not linked by connectives like 'while' or 'and', which would indicate the relationship of one to another. Such connectives would relate the sentences in particular grammatical patterns, whereas 'paratactic' construction simply leaves such relationships unspecified. The opening sentence of the passage just quoted provides a striking example. This repeated occurrence of subject and verb creates a sense of activity even when the human protagonist is immobile.[9] Charlotte Brontë's frequent use of personification similarly contributes to the dramatic style of the novel: even the internal processes of thought and feeling are dramatized and made concrete by this device. Here is perhaps the most famous instance:

> conscience, turned tyrant, held passion by the throat, told her, tauntingly, she had yet but dipped her dainty foot in the slough, and swore that with that arm of iron, he would thrust her down to unsounded depths of agony. (Ch. 27, p. 301)

As I have already said, there is some overlap between the two approaches – the linguistic analysis conducted by Margot Peters, which I have drawn on above, includes 'personification', a feature which would certainly be included in some traditional readings. But where these readings would concentrate on *interpreting* specific examples of the figure, the linguistic approach focuses on the characteristic effect of *all* such figures. Such an approach is less successful in bringing out specific effects and meanings, but it is helpful as a means of locating the characteristic language uses which together give Charlotte Brontë's prose its particular 'flavour' – that intensely poetic style which it is easy to respond to, but more difficult to pin down and explain. This attention to the structural rather than the semantic aspects of the text is, I think, particularly effective as a means of explaining the paradoxical sense of energy and urgency in passages where there is no physical activity.

To sum up, then, the characteristics of the style of *Jane Eyre*: a prolific use of imagery, emotive adjectives and adverbs; inversions and a dramatic use of syntax; archaisms and latinisms. All these contribute to the 'poetic' quality of the prose, a prose that draws attention to itself. It is a literary style, rather than one based on the rhythms and vocabulary of colloquial speech. The dialogue is, indeed, often criticized for its remoteness from everyday speech. But *Jane Eyre* does not attempt to disguise itself as an oral account, often explicitly presenting itself as a written document. Its literariness therefore functions as a reminder that it should not be confused with a 'slice of life'.

A rather different view of the novel's language can be obtained by considering the concept of 'discourse structure' or 'mind-style'.[10] The distinction between 'text' and 'discourse' is the basis of modern literary linguistics. 'Text' refers to the actual disposition of the words on the page, the sequence of sentences which leads the eye from left to right across the 'information structure' of the passage, allowing the reader to retrieve information in sequence. 'Discourse', on the other hand, is defined as 'the indication in language structure of the author's beliefs, the character of his thought-processes'. This includes such traditional concepts as point of view, but analysed linguistically:

for instance, it has been pointed out that verbs like 'seem' and 'feel' are used to indicate a point of view external to a character, from which that character's feelings are presented. 'He seemed happy' is a simple example where 'seemed' implies observation and critical analysis rather than inside information: it offers the possibility that 'he' was self-deceived, or actively putting on an appearance of happiness, as in 'he seemed happy, but to a careful observer it was clear that there was something troubling him'. It is important to note that we are here looking for the author's 'beliefs', not in feelings or ideas articulated by the characters, or even the narrator, but in the linguistic structures used – not in *what* is said, but in *how* it is said.

'Discourse structure' or 'mind-style', then, is any distinctive linguistic presentation of an individual character's mental state, to be explored through the vocabulary, phraseology and syntax of that character, whether in thought or in dialogue. You will notice that this approach includes both semantic and structural features of the text. It has been suggested that 'mind-style' is largely determined by the underlying conception of 'agency and animacy' – the character's understanding of causation, of who or what is responsible for events.[11]

I would like you to read the following passage from *Jane Eyre* in the light of this theory of 'mind discourse'. Who or what does Jane perceive to be controlling events? How does Jane represent her feelings?

> My hopes were all dead – struck with a subtle doom, such as, in one night, fell on all the first-born in the land of Egypt. I looked on my cherished wishes, yesterday so blooming and glowing; they lay stark, chill, livid – corpses that could never revive. I looked at my love: that feeling which was my master's – which he had created; it shivered in my heart, like a suffering child in a cold cradle; sickness and anguish had seized it: it could not seek Mr Rochester's arms – it could not derive warmth from his breast. Oh, never more could it turn to him; for faith was blighted, – confidence destroyed! Mr Rochester was not to me what he had been; for he was not what I had thought him. I would not ascribe vice to him; I would not say he had betrayed me: but the attribute of stainless truth was gone from his idea; and from his presence I must go: *that* I perceived well. (Ch. 26, pp. 298–9)

DISCUSSION

As in the conscience/passion passage, Jane employs personification, presenting her wishes as corpses, her love as a 'suffering child'. Apart from giving the passage a visual quality, and increasing its emotional intensity, these personifications suggest her feelings have an existence separate from herself. Phrases like 'it could not seek Mr Rochester's arms', rather than '*I* could not seek Mr Rochester's arms', convey a degree of detachment on Jane's part which raises it above self-pity. But does it not also convey a lack of control? That first clause – 'My hopes were all dead' – is a nominalization, a transformation of the verb 'I hoped' into the noun 'hopes'. Such nominalizations allow the emotions to be presented as concrete presences, separable from the character rather than inherent. They also suggest inactivity by repressing the agency function: that is, they repress the fact that Jane is the agent, the 'I' who hopes. Another characteristic of Jane's syntax here is the use of the passive – 'faith was blighted–confidence destroyed' – and the frequency with which she is the object of the sentence, rather than its subject: 'Mr Rochester was not to me . . . would hurry me . . . would want me'. There are relatively few sentences in which Jane is the subject, the 'I', rather surprising in a passage exploring the narrator's own feelings. Even her love is seen as an object 'created' by her 'master' and compared to a child. The implication is that Jane is overwhelmingly conscious of her own helplessness, before both her own feelings and her situation.

But is this one example of Jane's discourse enough from which to draw conclusions about her 'mind-style'? Or does it simply indicate her state of mind at this point in the novel? Re-read the end of this chapter (which concludes Volume II), and the end of Ch. 15 (which concludes Volume I). Do these passages have anything in common stylistically? Do they appear to represent similar mental states?

DISCUSSION

On many occasions Jane explicitly expresses her dislike of losing control, even – or perhaps particularly – when it is the prospect of being 'dressed like a doll by Mr Rochester' (Ch. 24, p. 271). She also dislikes being viewed as an object, as you may remember from her description of being marked out as a liar at Lowood (Ch. 7, pp. 67–8). I think you will agree that the passage which ends Volume I is remarkably similar to the end of Volume II, both in the use of the flood imagery mentioned earlier in this chapter, and the kind of syntax discussed above. The language of each suggests loss of control, by both semantic and syntactic means.

We shall be returning to this kind of linguistic analysis when we discuss the novel's ending in the next chapter and in Chapter 6. You can prepare for the first of these discussions by comparing the

language and syntax in which Jane describes her marriage (Ch. 38, p. 456) with that of the extract we've just discussed. Whom or what does she present as agent here? Here are some more passages which you could analyse for yourselves along the lines suggested by this chapter.
(1) 'Night was come . . . and looked round me' (Ch. 28, pp. 328–9). You will have little difficulty registering the religious vocabulary used here, but can you find any echoes of Biblical syntax? Or any echoes of the allegorical style of Bunyan's *Pilgrim's Progress*? Notice, for instance, the personification of Want.
(2) 'Don't imagine such hard things . . . peace' (Ch. 32, p. 377–8). This is Rivers speaking. What evidence can you find here of the same sense of being out of control implied by Jane's language on pages 298–9? Remember to look for the linguistic structures that convey this. In what way is such language appropriate here?
(3) 'I *can* do what he wants . . . grudging.' (Ch. 34, p. 409). By what linguistic means does Charlotte Brontë convey Jane's internal conflict? What structures does she use to convey the to and fro of her arguments?

As you work through the exercises in the following chapters, try to put into practice what you have learned from this brief introduction to linguistic analysis, since it will in many cases provide additional pointers to the effect of a passage. It will in every case contribute to your understanding of the way its effects are achieved, since an understanding of the basic structures which enable any single instance of language use to have meaning increases our responsiveness to the important effects of variations in those structures.

4. Realism or Romance?

You should by now have read, in conjunction with this *Guide*, all of the novel dealing with Gateshead, Lowood and Thornfield. This chapter relates to all three sections, although it pays particular attention to Ch. 27 (pp. 301–26), which we have not yet dealt with in any detail. I will also ask you to look ahead to the final chapters, in order to assess the degree of 'realism' or 'romance' which attaches to the novel's ending.

'Realism' is a term which has too many different and complex meanings to go into here. To avoid confusion, I shall use the term to denote the trend in nineteenth-century fiction, recently described as 'classic realism',[1] which, it has been claimed, is clearly exemplified in novels like George Eliot's *Middlemarch*. This trend, however, can be traced back to the eighteenth century, where it originated as a reaction, in writers like Richardson and Fielding, to the earlier romance. As part of the wider cultural changes that accompanied the rise of a new middle-class reading public, this reaction involved a movement away from previous literary practice, with its emphasis on 'universals' to innovation and the individual experience.[2] At the risk of over-simplification, therefore, 'realism' and 'romance' can usefully be defined in opposition to each other. 'Realism' aims at fidelity to everyday domestic life, whereas 'romance' deals with life's more heroic aspects, aiming at idealization. 'Realism' is therefore usually concerned with a much wider social range than the courtly world of most 'romance'. 'Realism' is about the ordinary and contemporary, whereas 'romance' is about the *extra*ordinary, often presented in a historical setting. 'Realism' aims at plausibility, seeking rational explanations for all events; 'romance' includes the mythical or supernatural in its vision of life.

In the essay quoted earlier on pp. 27–8, however, David Lodge argues that the language of *Jane Eyre*, through its easy movement from the literal to the symbolic, fuses the realistic and the romantic. Charlotte Brontë similarly combines all the 'romance' elements – such as the lunatic concealed in the attic – with the attention to physical and psychological detail more typical of 'realism'. How does she succeed in bringing together two apparently contrasted modes of writing?

It has long been recognized that 'romance', however improbable in the way of ordinary life, may embody psychic truths which cannot be expressed within the terms of everyday reality. Charlotte Brontë was clearly aware of this when she wrote to the critic, George Henry Lewes in 1848: 'Miss Austen being, as you say, without "sentiment", without *poetry*, maybe *is* sensible, real (more *real* than *true*), but she cannot be great.'[3] Robert Heilman suggests that, in her search for truth, the novelist used and modified many of the conventions of Gothic romance, a form popular late in the eighteenth and early in the nineteenth century. These tales of mystery and terror, often set in an ancient and haunted house, used many supernatural elements. At its best, the form was used to articulate new kinds of feeling, areas of feeling precluded by the realist convention. Heilman argues that Charlotte Brontë found new ways to achieve the same end: Jane's dreams and drawings, for instance, are symbolic representations through which the author plumbs the heroine's psyche, rather than simply thrilling additions to the drama. The novel rehabilitates the extra-rational, as Gothic had sometimes done, but within a framework of the less familiar realities of human life, rather than through the marvellous.[4]

But no one was more aware of the limitations of romance than Charlotte Brontë herself. Her earliest fiction had been written in collaboration with her brother, Branwell. Together they invented the amoral fantasy world of Angria, and their *Legends of Angria*, written between 1834 and 1839, allowed total freedom to the imagination and the emotions. In consequence, however, these stories evaded the need to examine the real social and moral issues which concerned her. Romance allows for solutions even when there are no resolutions of the conflicts involved. Before she came to write *Jane Eyre*, therefore, she had abandoned this world, expressing her feelings in these terms:

> I long to quit for awhile (sic) that burning clime where we have sojourned too long – its skies flame – the glow of sunset is always upon it – the mind would cease from excitement and turn now to a cooler region where the dawn breaks grey and sober, and the coming day for a time at least is subdued by clouds.[5]

In her first novel, *The Professor*, written in 1846, Charlotte Brontë strove for what she calls in her Preface 'plain and homely' realism. But in *Jane Eyre*, she opted for a union of 'realism' and 'romance' which could articulate the conflict in her work between the 'plain and homely' and the extraordinary, between morality and passion.

There are romance elements in the Moor House section of the novel: Jane's discovery of her inheritance and kinship with the Rivers family clearly belongs to the tradition of fairy tale. Nevertheless, it is Rochester and all that relates to him, which have been the most frequent target for criticism of the romance aspect of the novel.

Many critics have seen Rochester as a mere fantasy figure.[6] When reading Jane's description of Rochester's grim, dark face, his piercing eyes, his rugged features and his equally rugged manners, it is certainly tempting to see him as a literary stereotype of the kind to be found in much contemporary fiction written for women's magazines. But we have to remember that *Jane Eyre* played a large part in creating that particular stereotype. As far as Charlotte Brontë's own literary development is concerned, Rochester represents a break with the handsome hero of tradition, as found in her Angrian fiction. More specific criticisms relate Rochester to Byron: a contemporary review refers to a 'shade of Byronic gloom and appetising mystery'.[7] What exactly is implied by this comparison?

The popular conception of the Byronic hero is of a rebel, dark and compelling in appearance, though not handsome: a man who exercises considerable charm over women in spite of – or because of? – a guilty secret from which he is trying to escape. One of the most typical of Byron's heroes is Cain. His story will be familiar to you from the Bible, even if you have never read any of Byron's poems. Charlotte Brontë herself described Byron's *Cain* as a 'magnificent poem', although she had some reservations about recommending it to her friend Ellen Nussey.[8] Cain is condemned to roam the earth, an outcast, for killing his brother. In his poem, Byron presents Cain as an unhappy and isolated man even before the murder. Too proud to accept God's authority, he is resentful at being punished for the sins of his parents.

Would you now re-read Rochester's account of his past in Ch. 20 (p. 220) and Ch. 27 (pp. 301–326). What evidence can you find that he is conceived in terms of the Byronic model? Is there other evidence to the contrary?

DISCUSSION

Rochester refutes any suggestion that he has commited a crime, acknowledging only an error, for which he blames his father (see p. 220). He describes his wanderings in exile after his marriage, using his unhappiness as justification for 'overleaping an obstacle of custom' which his own judgment does not accept as an impediment. Chapter 27 reiterates the idea that he was a victim while retaining the other Byronic elements: he sees himself as 'burdened' with a 'curse' and opposes his 'rational' justification to divine law. But Rochester does not inhabit the morally chaotic universe of the Angrian heroes, and there are differences which transform him from the Byronic stereotype. Notice, for instance, his 'scruple' about confining his wife in the unhealthy climate of Ferndean (p. 304). Notice, too, that he describes Bertha as a woman 'in the style of Blanche Ingram' (p. 309). The suggested similarity indicates that by the time he meets Jane, he has learned enough not to repeat his earlier mistake of marrying for money or social considerations.

Nevertheless, we need to establish Jane's attitude to such Byronic, romance elements as there evidently are in Rochester. Is she attracted by them? Is he, as some critics have suggested, the embodiment of a 'true woman's longing . . . for a strong master'?[9] Re-read Jane's description of her first meeting with Rochester (Ch. 12, pp. 113–4), and compare it with Rochester's account (Ch. 13, p. 123). What similarities and differences do you notice? Turning again to Ch. 27, are there any differences in the attitudes each of them displays towards Bertha (see pp. 305–14)? And what do Rochester's plans for a new life suggest about *his* grasp of reality (see p. 308)?

DISCUSSION

Rochester appears just as Jane's imagination is preparing her for a creature from fairy tale, so that at first she sees 'a lion-like creature with long hair and a huge head', which turns out to be his dog. But the minute reality intrudes, her fantasies dissolve: 'The man, the human being, broke the spell at once.' (p. 113.) Rochester similarly thinks 'unaccountably of fairy tales'; but unlike Jane he returns to and elaborates the fairy image, most notably in his conversation with Jane and Adèle after Jane has agreed to marry him (Ch. 24, p. 270). In spite of Adèle's childish insistence on reality, on 'mademoiselle', Rochester persists in depicting their relationship in terms of fairy enchantment. Where Jane readily adjusts her romantic imaginings to reality, Rochester tries to evade reality through his romanticizing. He projects a Byronic image as a means of self-justification.

In describing Bertha, Rochester uses terms which enhance the Gothic horror of his situation: she is a 'wild beast' locked in a 'goblin's cell' (p. 313). When he talks of his wife's 'familiar', Jane reproaches him: 'you are inexorable for that unfortunate lady: you speak of her with hate – with vindictive antipathy. It is cruel – she cannot help being mad.' (p. 305.) In his eagerness to distance himself from Bertha, he denies her humanity as he similarly denies that of his former mistresses. He thinks he can shed his Byronic past by simply abandoning the Gothic world of Thornfield. Thus he plans to make Jane his wife in *his* eyes, if no-one else's, in 'a white-walled villa on the shores of the Mediterranean'. He is still romanticizing, evading reality by creating a fantasy world expressing his own needs. The more richly he develops these fantasies, the more Jane resists. Rochester has to abandon this fantasy world, to grow out of the Byronic mould, before he can finally be united with Jane. The Byronic associations of his character are used, therefore, not so much to define him as to suggest his self-dramatizing tendency, which the 'realistic' elements in Jane's character and the rest of the novel serve to criticize and evaluate. The seriousness of Charlotte Brontë's 'Farewell to Angria' is most evident in the presentation of Jane herself. For the centre of the novel's focus is not the powerful Byronic male, but a powerless young female – a *plain* young female. Why is Jane's plainness so insisted on by herself as much as by her author? In the conversation between Jane and Rochester in Ch. 24 (pp. 260–4), Jane not only insists on her lack of beauty – 'I am your plain, Quakerish governess' – but rejects all Rochester's attempts to beautify her with jewels, satin and lace. It is not simply that such things are alien to her taste, but that she feels they are alien to her *self*. If Rochester were to succeed in changing her in this way, she would no longer be Jane Eyre, but 'an ape in a harlequin's jacket'. 'I will be myself', she insists. Through Jane's plainness Charlotte Brontë is deliberately defying the Romantic convention that all heroines are beautiful.

> 'She once told her sisters that they were wrong – even morally wrong – in making their heroines beautiful as a matter of course. They replied that it was impossible to make a heroine interesting on any other terms. Her answer was, "I will prove to you that you are wrong; I will show you a heroine as plain and as small as myself, who shall be as interesting as any of yours."'[10]

Several aspects of Jane's *character* evidently break with the Romantic female stereotype too. For example: her refusal to

Charlotte Brontë by her brother, Branwell (National Portrait Gallery).

acquiesce in the 'wisdom' of those in positions of authority, whether it be the authority of age (Mrs Reed), social position (Rochester), religion (Brocklehurst and Rivers), or sex (Rochester again). Linked with this characteristic is her outspokenness, and her sense of equality with everyone she meets, even when arriving at Moor House as a destitute beggar (see Ch. 28, pp. 339–42). She is further aided in her independence by a sense of intellectual and moral power which she relies upon in all her battles with those who try to force her into passivity and acquiescence. More generally, we can add that as a child Jane is constantly criticized for being un-childlike, for the same characteristics which are later condemned as 'unfeminine'. This indicates the childlike demeanor considered appropriate in young women. At Lowood she learns to control her outspokenness and acquires 'discipline', so that she is able to fulfil her role as governess adequately. Her less conventional qualities are, nevertheless, what attract Rochester's attention. But consider his reaction to Jane's refusal to leave Thornfield with him (Ch. 27, p. 306). What is Rochester's evaluation here? Bearing in mind the stereotyped hero and heroine of romance – the helpless woman, emotionally and physically dependent on the strong and purposeful male, always in complete control of the situation – does this scene subvert these stereotypes in any way?

DISCUSSION

In this scene Jane needs all her courage to resist the man she loves. But this courage, which so impressed Rochester when employed to save him from fire and prevent Mason from bleeding to death, becomes here, in his eyes, 'the hitch in Jane's character'. Her independent spirit and unwillingness to say what pleases are not appreciated. The qualities which won Rochester's love and respect are, it appears, to be rejected as soon as they become inconvenient.

The scene, moreover, reverses conventional sexual roles and stereotypes. It is the male who is overcome by his feelings, while Jane remains rational. The only time she betrays the feelings which are undoubtedly present is when she deliberately weeps, as a means of achieving a desired effect on Rochester. This act of manipulation is not, however, callous; it is simply an attempt to retain control of the situation by the only means available to her – 'an inward power; a sense of influence'. Rochester has every advantage on his side – wealth, social position, her love for him, and his sheer physical strength. Charlotte Brontë does not attempt to conceal the realities of the power relations represented: the threat of rape is evident in Rochester's threat of violence and Jane's fear of his 'wild licence'. But Jane has the moral advantage and the wit to use it. The 'charm' of the situation for her is a further reminder of her unconventional pleasure in exercising her 'powers' like this. The opposition between 'realism' and 'romance' is, therefore, very consciously maintained in a relationship which breaks so completely with conventional conceptions of courtship.

So far I have used the terms 'realism' and 'romance' as convenient ways of differentiating contrasting aspects of the novel. But I would now like to look more closely at the term 'realism'. In the first place, 'realism' is not 'reality', whatever that might be. I have said very little about the relationship between Lowood and Cowan Bridge, the 'reality' on which the fictional institution was based. This is partly because of my own reservations about the usefulness of biographical information to a first reading of the novel (see Chapter 8 of this *Guide*). But more important are the dangers involved in suggesting that the Lowood section is 'realistic' simply because it is based on real life. It is just as possible to write 'realistically' about something that never took place as it is to write about real-life events in such a way as to make them seem fantastic.

But in a novel like *Jane Eyre* the idea that its 'realism' derives from its basis in 'reality' is very seductive, since it lays claim to being autobiographical, a true account of the narrator's experience. If you are using the World's Classics edition of the novel, you will see from the frontispiece that the original read '*Jane Eyre: An Autobiography*. Edited by Currer Bell.' The word 'edited', meaning 'prepared for print by another person', introduces the idea of an intermediary – the 'editor' Currer Bell – who is ready to vouch for the authenticity of the document he is presenting to the public. It further encourages the illusion that the book presents a true story. Having considered the presentation of that 'truth', however, in terms of both realism and romance, we have to be aware that what we refer to as 'realism' is as much a question of method as of content. The suffix '-ism' alerts us to the fact that 'realism', just as much as 'romance', is a series of literary conventions, a fictional method which creates an *illusion* of reality.

The concept of 'mimetic realism', the idea that realism is, or could be, an *imitation* of reality has been seriously challenged by recent criticism, as we saw in Chapter 2 of this *Guide* (pp. 17–20). Such criticism has drawn attention to the wide gulf between any literary work, which is purely verbal, and the largely non-verbal nature of reality. Even dialogue, which appears to come closest to the 'real thing', is conventionalized in realist fiction, as anyone who has tried to take a transcript of an actual conversation can testify. Structuralist and post-structuralist criticism has forced us to adopt a more analytical approach to a mode of writing so central to our popular culture, so familiar to us, that we tend to view it as the 'natural' way to write about the 'real' world. It has also called into question the apparent objectivity of nineteenth-century realism. What is easily seen as a portrait of society as it *was* is now more often seen as a view of society as the author saw it – a view, moreover, inevitably affected by the ideology of that society. The further implications of this view will be discussed in Chapter 8 below.

But to return to Jane's relationship with Rochester, does this 'romance' compromise what might be called Jane's feminist aspirations? Jane's insistence on being herself even as she prepares to become Mrs Rochester suggests that her desire for autonomy is equally as important as the 'love story' dimension of the novel. Indeed, the love story is a vehicle for her search for identity. How are the two quests, for independence and inter-dependence, reconciled?

Let us begin by considering Jane's reasons for leaving Rochester when she discovers he is already married. We again need to look closely at Chapter 27, and her feelings before and after Rochester's attempts to exonerate himself. George Eliot commented on this episode as follows: 'All self-sacrifice is good – but one could like it to be in a somewhat nobler cause than that of a diabolical law which chains a man body and soul to a putrefying carcase'.[11] Was she correct in attributing Jane's action to respect for conventional morality? What *are* Jane's reasons? The answer lies perhaps in the implicit warning Rochester himself gives as to the possible consequences of staying. Read his account of life with Céline Varens and his other mistresses (pp. 315–6).

DISCUSSION

To deal with George Eliot's judgment first, if conventional morality alone had such a hold on Jane, would she find it so easy to forgive him as she does (see p. 302), even before she hears what he has to say in his own defence? Would we not expect to find her repelled, rather than as strongly attracted as ever? Jane feels that *good* could result from her staying with him: her 'very Conscience and Reason . . . charged [her] with crime in resisting him' (p. 321) and thus condemning him to a life of dissolution. But she does admit to taking to heart Rochester's implied warning: 'Hiring a mistress is the next worse thing to buying a slave: both are often by nature, and always by position, inferior; and to live familiarly with inferiors is degrading' (p. 316). Rochester himself appears conscious of the dilemma involved: 'it is you, spirit – with will and energy, and virtue and purity – that I want: not alone your brittle frame' (p. 322). In spite of the anger he previously expressed over Jane's obstinacy, he is aware that it is what is exceptional about Jane that he desires – her refusal to conform either to the conventional role of the young lady, or the equally conventional role of the fallen woman. When he describes their first meeting, he stresses her 'authority' and her 'fresh sap and sense' (p. 317), which would be violated if she were to accept his authority against her conscience.

Is Jane, then, acting on purely pragmatic grounds, weighing a possible brief period of happiness against a possible future of misery? This possibility gains little support from the way Jane's reactions are presented in this chapter. The sense of conflict and the delirium of Jane's departure point to a motivation more deeply felt. The real answer is, I suggest, given by Jane herself when Rochester urges his need of her against the lack of concern anyone else will feel about her choice: '*I* care for myself. The more solitary, the more friendless, the more unsustained I am, the more I will respect myself.' (p. 321.) Self-respect, a belief in her own integrity, is what finally proves strongest. The fact that there are no witnesses should be sufficient indication that 'self-respect' does not, moreover, mean holding one's head high in front of the neighbours. For it is true that ultimately no one cares whether Jane is true to herself. And no one is as aware as Jane of how far her feelings can threaten that self. Her dream of the Red Room (p. 323) is a reminder of the loss of consciousness, of identity, which follows abandonment to intense feeling and visions born of the imagination. Rochester is asking her to be led both by passion and by a Romantic vision which denies the reality of his marriage. He is asking her to surrender her view of herself and the world for his. Mark Kinkead-Weekes sums up the place of love in the novel like this: the self can only be fulfilled through love, but that love must be between two individuals, sure of their own identity and content to let the integrity of the other remain intact.[12]

So long as Rochester respects Jane's integrity, he gives her a sense of equality which her experience as a social inferior makes her respond to with delight. But she persists in calling him 'Master', and her repeated use of the term 'obedience' (see below, Chapter 6 pp. 64–5) seems to undermine the idea of equality. Jane's readiness to 'serve' Rochester appears to reinforce the convention of the submissive, dutiful wife. But in saying, 'I obeyed', Jane remains the agent, linguistically speaking, as I suggested earlier. She uses the phrase, I think, to suggest a conscious act, rather than helpless, unthinking passivity. While ultimately implying submission, the phrase nevertheless foregrounds the subject's consciousness: stemming from the Latin *obedire*, meaning 'to give ear, hearken', it draws attention first to the act of hearing, and secondly to the element of free choice which lies in the possibility of *disobedience*. When she tells Rochester, in Ch. 27 (p. 320), that to obey him *now* would be wrong, she makes that previous intimation of choice a present reality.

But we cannot assess the degree of equality represented by Jane's relationship with Rochester without looking ahead to the novel's ending. Critical interpretations of the final chapters are various and conflicting. What was your view of it? Would you agree with such a critic as Robert Martin who sees it as an unequivocally happy ending, comparable to the end of *Paradise Lost*, where Adam and Eve enter a new life?[13] For him Jane's Conclusion expresses complete happiness. Or would you see force in the opposite view of Richard Chase, who sees Jane transformed in these closing pages into the stereotyped wife whose image she had previously rejected so strenuously? Chase suggests, like D. H. Lawrence before him, that the marriage also requires the taming of Rochester, his mutilation and blindness acting as a symbolic castration.[14] Would you agree with another commentator, Annette Tromly, who challenges the idea that Ferndean represents a Miltonic Eden? She suggests that such a view overlooks the many ironies of this location: not only too 'insalubrious' even for Bertha, but totally enclosed and cut off from the rest of the world, in direct contrast to the ending of *Paradise Lost*, where the 'world was all before' Adam and Eve.[15] I shall leave you to consider which of these readings approximates most closely to your own, until we discuss the novel's ending in relation to the work as a whole in the next chapter.

I want now, however, to consider one interpretation, from a feminist viewpoint, as it raises very effectively the issues with which the ending confronts us, particularly the question of whether it represents a 'realist' or 'romance' solution. Helene Moglen identifies the threat represented by Rochester in these terms: whereas he is in a position of great freedom, in spite of his previous marriage, Jane's life has created in her a need for the kind of symbiotic relationship of emotional interdependency which is the basis of middle-class patriarchy,[16] justified by the myth of Romantic love. Her argument takes us back to Byron, who represented an ideal of psychic and social freedom for Charlotte Brontë, but with whom she could not identify because she was a woman. For a woman the reality behind the Byronic myth was this:

> Once scrutinised, the myth discloses those economic and social forces which determine the nature of psychosexual interaction. The advent of industrialization and the growth of the middle class was accompanied by a more diffuse yet more virulent form of patriarchy than any that had existed before. As men became uniquely responsible for the support of the family, women became 'possessions', identified with their 'masters'' wealth. The status of the male owner derived from the extent of his woman's leisure time and the degree of her emotional and physical dependence upon him. Sexual relationships followed a similar pattern of dominance and submission.[17]

Please read Chs 37 and 38 (pp. 435–58) in the light of Moglen's argument. Does it explain the kind of relationship represented in Jane's marriage to your satisfaction? Does Jane remain caught up in this patriarchial myth? Or have sufficient changes taken place in Rochester and their relationship to enable them to achieve a truly equal partnership? As you read Ch. 38, pay particular attention to the language, bearing in mind our linguistic analysis of pp. 298–9 in the previous chapter. Compare p. 456 with these earlier pages. Who or what is the predominant grammatical subject here?

DISCUSSION

On first seeing Rochester again, Jane notices the change in his appearance: she calls him a 'sightless Samson' (p. 436), his power circumscribed but his ferocity increased. What of his former romantic tendencies? At first he again conceives of Jane as a 'fairy' (p. 441), her presence as an 'enchantment' (p. 442), but this time it is because the reality of her presence seems too miraculous to believe in. He is now fearful of being misled by his romantic imaginings. It is Jane's emphatic realism – her talk of money matters, his ugliness and the need to 're-humanize' him – which convinces him that she is not a product of his imagination. The romantic creations of his former self no longer come between them.

As for their relationship, Jane is now independent financially; she has acquired a family and a position in life. In this sense, then, she is more equal to Rochester. But it appears that Rochester's sexual dominance has also to be subdued. Her tormenting of Rochester with the handsome figure of Rivers is surely a conscious re-working of

Rochester's use of Blanche Ingram to arouse Jane's jealousy. Rochester's physical mutilation clearly makes this reversal of roles easier: her hand 'prisons' his, holding it in 'custody'. In his blindness she functions as his eyes, interpreting the world for him when they walk out into the woods. Is she now imposing her view of the world on him, as he formerly sought to impose his on her? Jane's view of the situation is this: 'I love you better now, when I can be really useful to you' (p. 451).

When we come to Ch. 38, from the very active assertion which opens the chapter – 'Reader, I married him' – Jane presents herself as very much the agent of her own destiny. Comparing p. 456 with pp. 298 and 299, I noticed how many of the sentences begin with 'I', with Jane as subject. The simple statement of fact, 'I have been married for ten years', is followed by 'I know . . .' and 'I hold myself . . .': there is no hesitation here about expressing her own judgments. Emotion is expressed as knowledge, as rational certainties: the simply assertive 'is' and 'are' are used repeatedly. The only other agent is 'he', Rochester, the more frequent 'We' asserting his identity and equality with 'I', Jane. The parallel constructions of the syntax endorse this union of identities: 'I know no weariness of my Edward's society: he knows none of mine . . . . All my confidence is bestowed on him; all his confidence is devoted to me'. Every statement expresses confidence, a sense of control of both herself and her situation.

Annette Tromly is suspicious of this description, feeling it 'betrays the same complacency that she has confronted in other people so often. She speaks glibly on behalf of her husband; her repeated assertions that they are one have the effect of making Rochester disappear'.[18] You will have to decide for yourself whether you share this suspicion, or whether you regard this marriage as representing a genuine achievement of equality after a sustained struggle on Jane's part against herself and the outside world. I would only add that this resolution perhaps continues the novel's opposition of realistic/romantic views of sexual relations, by suggesting the limitations of 'reality'. Perhaps this marriage should be seen not as simply the conventional happy ending, but as an acknowledgment of the limitations Victorian society imposed on female aspirations. Furthermore, while Ferndean may not be a Paradise, it is clearly disengaged from the social world we have glimpsed in Rochester's relationship with Blanche Ingram, or from that kind of 'normal' life, involving participation in the community, which Jane entered on briefly at Moor House. The withdrawn nature of their situation is, therefore, a tacit acknowledgment that their relationship is not typical of their society, and can perhaps only survive outside society. Where marriage is conventionally in Victorian novels a sign of resolution and accommodation with social norms, this marriage signifies a more qualified and complex kind of resolution.

5. Structure and Theme

If you have not already done so, you should read to the end of the novel before tackling this and subsequent chapters of the *Guide*.

* * *

What do we mean when we talk about 'structure' in a novel? Linguistics again provides a useful analogue. I referred in Chapter 3 to 'the structures which enable the individual words or lexical items to have meaning' (p. 32). Meaning is relational, not substantial. That is, it is not to be found in the individual lexical items or 'signs' that constitute a sentence, but in the relationship *between* the signs. If we compare the sentence 'I saw a blue car' with the sentence 'I saw a blue movie', we can see that the meaning of the sign 'blue' changes, depending on its context. And so with the novel: meaning is to be found not in its individual elements – however we choose to break those down – but in the *relationship* between them. 'Structure' in the novel can, therefore, be defined as a perceived pattern of relationships. But the novel is, of course, a far more complex verbal form than a sentence, so that the possibilities of relationship are far greater. We can perceive many different structures in a text, depending on which aspects of the text we are considering – characters, imagery, location, can all perform a structuring function.

And the perception of any structure, any pattern, in the novel is an interpretative act, by which the reader makes connections within the text, and maintains those connections are significant. It constitutes a 'reading' of a novel, an interpretation of its *themes* – a subject I will return to later in this chapter.

Let us consider some of the implications of our discussion so far. If structure is a matter of the *reader*'s perception of relationship, then it follows both that different readers may perceive different structures in the same text, and that the *same* reader may, at different times, perceive more than one structure. Furthermore, the possibility of multiple structures opens up the possibility of *conflicting* or *contradictory* structures within the same text. And if a perception of structure involves a 'reading' of the text, then it becomes clearer why the same text should give rise to such a variety of critical interpretation. I shall be looking at some of these readings in this and the next chapter, but it needs to be stressed that, although I have drawn on structural linguistics for my analogue, structuralist *literary critics* are not concerned with interpreting the individual text in this way, so much as with identifying the basic structures which enable *all* texts to have meaning. Structures such as that of binary opposition (see pp. 19 and 57 of this *Guide*) would come into this category. I, however, will also be concerned in this chapter with more traditional approaches to structure and theme.

Many literary critics have, in fact, tended to talk as if a novel had a single 'structure', and indeed, are apt to insist that their sense of the structure is the one that really matters. The previous paragraph has indicated the arguments against such a position, but this does not invalidate all that has been written from this angle, particularly as regards what might be called the novel's 'objective structure'. By this I mean the arrangement of events in a novel according to a time-scale, a chronology. This 'objectivity' is really a product of a culture that sees 'time' in this way: fiction that plays around with the idea of time, as H. G. Wells does in his *The Time Machine* (1895), and as some contemporary science-fiction does, disturbs a deep-seated cultural agreement and challenges our sense of what constitutes 'the real'. But I want to retain the term 'objective' as a useful way of indicating a structure involving a set of relationships which can be objectively verified: we can plot the sequence of chapters against a calendar or clock. This 'time-structure', to give it another name, is the commonest type of structure analysed by critics who conceive of the novel as having a unitary structure.

Consider the rhyme, *Solomon Grundy*:

Solomon Grundy
Born on a Monday
Christened on Tuesday
Married on Wednesday
Took ill on Thursday
Worse on Friday
Died on Saturday
Buried on Sunday
  This is the end
  Of Solomon Grundy.

This deceptively simple narrative presents events in the sequence in which they occurred – 'and then and then and then' – so at first we might perceive an episodic or linear structure. But it does not take much thought to recognize further that a process of selection has taken place to determine which events in this life should be included, and how much of the narrative should be allocated to each. The absence of any reference to events between christening and marriage implies an uneventful period, from the narrator's point of view. What does this strict chronological sequence, emphasized by the use of successive days of the week, contribute to the poem? What, for instance, would be the difference if it began with Solomon's death, and narrated his life in flashback? We would lose the sense of these major events in his life following each other as rapidly and inexorably as the days of the week. As you can see, in *perceiving* the relationship between the lines as 'rapid' and 'inexorable', I am also *interpreting* the poem. If we go on to consider the poem's theme – the 'statement' it makes about life in general – my own reading leads me to suggest that its theme is the brevity of human life. However, you could also argue that the poem's theme is the idea that life has a shape and pattern of determinate time, and that the seven-day pattern of the poem implies its repeatability – that other lives will follow in the next week. You will notice that neither of these themes is *explicit* in the poem; these interpretations are only made possible by a structure of events which enables the reader to perceive meaning.[1]

In analysing structure in *Jane Eyre*, then, we can begin by considering its chronological structure. Like *Solomon Grundy*, the novel has an episodic structure, one phase of Jane's life following another in chronological sequence. But this sequence is disturbed at a number of points. Can you think of some examples? Try to identify at least three. What do you think are the reasons for them?

DISCUSSION

There are several departures from strict chronological sequence and here are some of the most emphatic: Rochester's accounts of his past (Ch. 15, pp. 141–6 and Ch. 27, pp. 309–19); Mrs Reed's death-bed retrospective (Ch. 21, pp. 233–4 and 240–42); Rivers's account of Jane's history as he knows it (Ch. 33, pp. 384–6); the ex-butler's account of the fire at Thornfield (Ch. 36, pp. 431–434). Did you light on any of these or others? And there is a principal 'formal' reason for them. Embedded as they are within Jane's tale they provide a means of telling us about past events without infringing the limits of Jane's experience and knowledge. This structure is, therefore, partly determined by the narrative method and the constraints of the first person narrator. This embedding, moreover, imposes effective limits on some of the potential sensationalism of the novel, specifically the exotic plot material relating to Bertha. Kathleen Tillotson sums it up like this:

> When the Angrian plot-material in *Jane Eyre* is recognized, its subordination is seen to be a triumph of structure and emphasis. Had the story begun with the nodal situation, we should have been on a distant island (Spanish Town standing for Glass Town or Verdopolis) and have seen Rochester's father and elder brother entrapping him into marriage with a vicious lunatic. Instead, this situation is imbedded in the main story, revealed retrospectively only at its climax; it is there not for its sensational sake, but as precisely that situation which will make Rochester's deception most nearly excusable, and Jane's resistance most difficult, producing the maximum of conflict between conscience and compassion and holding the reader's sympathies in true balance.[2]

The novel's chronological structure, therefore, exercises a degree of control over its 'romantic', emotional material. While on the one hand the novel's imagery may evoke elemental forces, on the other the chronological structure exerts a firm intellectual control which 'places' these feelings and experiences. As such, it articulates the tension between passion and reason which is one of the novel's principal themes.

Now let's move on to another 'structure', and the use of location as a structuring device. Because Jane moves from place to place, the reader is alerted to the possibility that such locational changes correspond to similar changes in the nature of Jane's experience. Each location represents a 'stage' both physical and experiential. Jane's passionate rebelliousness at Gateshead leads to her isolation and rejection. At Lowood, she learns to control this characteristic in order

ADVERTISEMENT

TO THE ILLUSTRATED EDITION OF THE

LIFE AND WORKS OF CHARLOTTE BRONTË

AND HER SISTERS.

THE descriptions in "Jane Eyre" and the other Fictions by Charlotte Brontë and her Sisters being mostly of actual places, the Publishers considered that Views would form the most suitable Illustrations of the Library Edition of the Novels. They are indebted for a clue to the real names of the most interesting scenes to a friend of the Misses Brontë, who has thus enabled the artist, Mr. E. M. Wimperis, to identify the places described. He made faithful sketches of them on the spot, and has also drawn them on wood; it is therefore hoped that these Views will add fresh interest to the reading of the Stories.

'Advertisement' to 1872 edition of *Jane Eyre*.

Drawing of Thornfield Hall by E. M. Wimperis, 1872 edition of *Jane Eyre*, Smith, Elder & Co.

to secure acceptance and affection. At Thornfield, Jane's passions are once more brought into play, by Rochester, but she is able to exercise the restraint of her conscience. Conscience alone, however, is found to provide inadequate motivation while Jane is at Moor House. Only at Ferndean can Jane find, through marriage to Rochester, a means of reconciling the demands of passion *and* conscience. Mark Kinkead-Weekes argues that the significance of these five locations – Gateshead, Lowood, Thornfield, Moor House and Ferndean – lies in the fact that each house is a metaphor for each of the stages which Jane's 'heart' has to pass through on its journey of self-discovery.[3] Bearing this in mind, we can now look at the link between location and imagery, which can be seen to provide a further structuring effect. In keeping with the basic fire/ice image-pattern, Gateshead and Lowood are both characterized by physical cold, but whereas the Red Room signifies the eruption of Jane's overheated emotions, Lowood is the place where she learns, at the fireside of Miss Temple, to discipline those feelings. Thornfield epitomizes warmth, both physical and emotional, and the attendant danger of all-consuming fire. Moor House is the location where Jane is most threatened by spiritual and emotional chill, while Ferndean is the scene of reconciliation – warmth without burning, the coolness of the evening air without the chill – once the fire of Thornfield has burnt itself out. This is a very schematic appraisal, but it should be useful in highlighting the basic structural outline.

Moreover, within this structure, the imagery has the further effect of pointing to certain thematic parallels. The Rivers family can be seen as a sort of revised version of the Reeds. They provide Jane with a sense of security and affection such as she never derived from her first 'family', but the repeated pattern of two sisters and one brother, the brothers sharing the same Christian name, alerts us to significant similarities. Both Mrs Reed and Rivers are characterized by ice, and there are surprising common elements in the presentation of John Reed and his apparently saintly Rivers counterpart. The literal meaning of their names suggests an association – reeds growing beside rivers – which is surely not accidental? Although St John's vocation, and the intensity of his dedication to it, make him an impressive figure in Jane's eyes, he attempts to bully Jane spiritually, as John Reed did physically; and both die (admittedly pursuing their very different ends) indifferent to the feelings of their families. I leave you to decide whether the similarities or differences are stronger.

While the imagery can be said to reinforce the five-part locational structure in this way, the dominant heat/cold contrast creates a simpler binary structure of opposites. Binary opposition, as we saw earlier, is one of the fundamental structures in our language, distinguishing male from female, night from day, black from white, right from wrong. In *Jane Eyre*, it is present in the imagery, in the thematic contrast of passion and reason, and in the characterization of Rochester as opposed to Rivers. You will notice that it cuts across the five-part locational structure, enabling the reader to perceive Jane's total experience as one of *conflict*, underlining the reading implied in our discussion of the time-structure. The five-part locational structure allows us to see a pattern of movement and growth, as we would expect of a *Bildungsroman*: as Jane moves from one location to another, she is confronted with different extremes – passion and reason, heat and cold – either within herself or in her environment. This pattern of extremes is reinforced by our perception of the binary structure. It is tempting, therefore, to see the five-part structure in terms of two pairs of opposites – Gateshead/Lowood, Thornfield/Moor House – leaving the numerically 'odd' fifth location, Ferndean. This fifth part of the structure then lends itself to being read as the point of resolution where opposing forces meet and are reconciled.

While such readings are attractively neat and clear, we need, however, always to be aware of their dangers. Are they *too* schematic? Do they derive from an unstated determination to impose an unambiguous shape upon the novel? – smoothing out, in the process, inconsistencies and contradictions? Let us consider now another structural view which allows for such contradiction.

As we read the novel, over and above our sense of progressing from one phase or location to another, we are also aware of moments of crisis or climax, moments which mark decisive turning-points in Jane's life. The first of these is Rochester's proposal that Jane should become his mistress (Chs 26 and 27). Here Jane has to choose between following the dictates of passion or the equally strong dictates of conscience. The crisis is particularly powerful, coming as it does after the carefully prepared climax of Jane's wedding day. The night before her wedding Jane expresses her own consciousness of the turning-point that marriage represents: of the child Adèle she says, 'She seemed the emblem of my past life; and he, I was now to array myself to meet, the dread, but adored, type of my unknown future day.' (Ch. 25, p. 289). In the event, of course, the threshold into sexual experience is not crossed.

The second crisis is provoked by St John's proposal of marriage (Chs 34 and 35, pp. 393–425). Compare this with Rochester's 'proposal'. What kind of threat do they represent to Jane? When and why does Jane come close to submitting to Rivers? Is this linked in any way with her earlier crisis with Rochester?

DISCUSSION

Presumably, most readers first notice the contrast between Rivers and Rochester. Rochester offers emotional and physical fulfilment, where Rivers advises Jane to abandon 'ties of the flesh' (p. 395). Rochester asks Jane to set aside divine law, standing between her and God; Rivers asks her to dedicate herself to God rather than himself, claiming she is 'formed for labour, not for love' (p. 407).

Yet aren't there also some striking similarities? Consider, for instance, Jane's description of learning 'Hindostanee' at Rivers's request. He is an 'exacting master'. Though Rivers is not Jane's employer as Rochester was, he assumes the same role of command and instruction. He also attempts to change Jane's nature as Rochester had done. To please him she would have to disown half her nature, just as Rochester requires her to abandon her moral sense. Her identity is to merge with his: 'A part of me you must become' (p. 413). He requires 'obedience' as Rochester does. Like Rochester, Rivers chooses Jane because she is not a conventional young lady, however much he is attracted to that type of woman as represented by Rosamond Oliver. And like Rochester he is nevertheless ready to condemn Jane for not accepting a properly submissive woman's role: her language in refusing him is, in his eyes, 'violent, unfeminine and untrue' (p. 417).

It is St John's sense of mission, his only genuine passion, which almost overwhelms Jane's sense of self: 'I felt veneration for St John – veneration so strong that its impetus thrust me at once to the point I had so long shunned. I was tempted to cease struggling with him – to rush down the torrent of his will into the gulf of his existence, and there lose my own.' Jane, moreover, explicitly recognizes the pattern being repeated: 'I was almost as hard beset by him now as I had been once before' (p. 423). Both men ask her to accept their view of herself and her destiny – a destiny of subservience to the male will – though one asks in the name of love, the other in the name of duty. Did you notice the torrent image, which echoes the imagery Jane uses for the despair which follows her non-marriage at the end of Volume II? In each case she is tempted to give up the struggle for her integrity, to allow herself to be overwhelmed. That is the threat which each suitor holds for her.

If we now look back at Jane's relationship with Helen Burns, we can see important parallels with the two options represented by Rochester and Rivers. As a young woman, Helen is a potential role model for Jane such as neither man can be, and Jane is impressed by the fortitude with which Helen bears her public punishment (Ch. 5, p. 52). But how much does she learn from Helen's example? Look again at this episode and at Jane's punishment (Ch. 7, pp. 67–8). What aspects of Helen's character appear to offer a positive model? Consider her philosophy (Ch. 6, pp. 55–9). Can you see any links between her otherwordliness and the presentation of St John Rivers?

DISCUSSION

Helen's virtues appear to be:

(1) Her determination to live by biblical precepts – 'the Bible bids us return good for evil' (p. 56).
(2) Her self-knowledge, demonstrated in her analysis of her own faults.
(3) Her self-control – she exhorts Jane, too, to forget the passionate emotions aroused by Mrs Reed.
(4) Her otherworldliness – 'I live in calm, looking to the end.' (p. 59) – and her belief in putting the love of God before everything else, even the love of other people.

But Jane appears to derive less from Helen's example than from her simple demonstration of affection in walking past the 'criminal' with a look and a smile. Once alone again, Jane's fortitude evaporates, and she is never able passively to endure injustice either for Helen or herself. Jane does learn from (3): she learns to control her emotions enough to be able to give Miss Temple a more restrained and therefore more plausible account of her life than she might otherwise have done. And the rest of her story demonstrates how much she has acquired of (2), self-knowledge. Her determination to live by biblical precepts, on the other hand, is always tempered by her independence in interpreting those precepts, often unconventionally.

But it is the influence of the last of these 'virtues', other-wordliness, that is most questionable. For it is through Jane's need for human love and affection that Helen has an influence on her. Starved of affection as a child, Jane is receptive to Helen out of her craving for a more positive human relationship. The nature of this influence is clarified upon Miss Temple's departure from Lowood. Under the influence of Miss Temple's friendship, Jane acquires self-discipline. Robbed of that presence, she returns to her 'natural element' (Ch. 10, p. 85). Both Helen and St John attempt to live their lives according to Christian principles and to subdue their more personal needs. And in telling Jane she is 'formed for labour, not for love', Rivers echoes Helen's warning against caring too much for human love. Above all, Helen fixes her eyes on the end of her earthly life, welcoming her early death as an escape from suffering and sin. Rivers, too, welcomes death in the words which end the novel, and in asking Jane to accompany him as a missionary he is in effect offering her, too, an early death, as she recognizes. But Jane opts for life, in every sense of the word, just as she opts for the life of human feeling rather than the death-in-life of Helen's other-wordliness.

I am suggesting, then, that Helen Burns presents Jane with her first 'proposal'. Jane's need for human affection and respect tempt her to adopt Helen's way as she is later tempted to adopt Rochester's or Rivers's. But in this earliest conflict, Jane is freed by Helen's death from the necessity of choosing. And because Helen is another woman, Jane is not threatened by male domination. The episode at Lowood, therefore, offers an experience of choice which Jane is able to make in relative freedom, as a kind of rehearsal for the far more difficult choices she will have to make in later life. I would suggest, furthermore, that this tri-partite structure of choices indicates an important theme – that of 'education' in the widest sense. Lowood school, Jane's role as governess and as teacher in the village school give objective expression to this theme, acting as images of the process by which Jane is brought to maturity and a secure sense of self. While ostensibly the teacher, Jane is effectually the taught: Rochester, her 'master' – an interestingly ambiguous term – and the cleric, Rivers, both attempt to indoctrinate her into their way of seeing, and in the process teach her something quite different.

If, as I have suggested, Helen, Rochester and Rivers are linked as would-be educators of Jane, this cuts across the reading implicit in the perception of a binary structure, with Rochester and Rivers as opposites. It also undermines the idea that a resolution of the conflict takes place in the 'fifth phase': it allows for the possibility that Jane's journey ends in compromise or regression, in the reunion with Rochester, a view we touched on in Chapter 4 of this *Guide* and will return to in Chapter 7.

We have already used the term 'theme' on a number of occasions, and I have argued that 'structure' makes possible the perception of theme. That is, our perception of patterns of similarity and contrast enables us to proceed from the particulars of the novel to a more general, abstract conception, by drawing our attention to the common element underlying those particulars. The idea of theme provides a conceptual overview to which the individual details of the text can be related, and by which their significance can be identified. If a novel can be said to bear a symbolic relationship to life, then 'theme' can be said to reside in that relationship: it is commonly held to *express* the relationship of the novel to life.

This, however, is not a view that would find sympathy among structuralist critics. According to structural linguistics, the relationship between a 'sign' and the concept it signifies is purely arbitrary: the French have a different sign, 'porte', for the same concept we signify with 'door'. And this sign 'door' can only have that meaning because it can be distinguished phonetically from other signs such as 'floor', 'dare', 'poor' etc. Its meaning derives, as we saw at the beginning of this chapter, from its 'syntagmatic' relationship with the other signs in the sentence, or utterance. But it also derives from its 'paradigmatic' relationship with every other word in the 'paradigm' or grammatical set to which it belongs. We understand 'door' not only because of its syntactic context, but because of the distinctions we draw between it and every other noun which could have occupied its place in the grammatical structure of the sentence. Meaning thus depends on the perception of *difference* as well as of relationship. Structuralist critics see the meaning of a text as similarly deriving from the relationship between its parts. But whereas, in linguistics, the sign 'door' and its signified, 'concept of door', have a *referent*, an actual door, a novel is a sign-system for which there is *no* specific set of referents. Critics like Barthes, therefore, argue that – since a novel is a sign-system whose meaning derives entirely from the relationship between the parts – the text has *no* referential function.[4] It cannot be 'about' life, only 'about' the nature of the text itself, or that of other texts. That is, it is primarily *self*-referential.

Nevertheless novels would hardly interest us if they did not bear, with whatever reservations and qualifications, upon 'life', and 'theme' remains a useful concept to represent that bearing. We have already touched on a number of possible themes in *Jane Eyre*: the conflict between reason and passion; education; moral growth. Let us look briefly at some further readings. Some critics see the novel in primarily religious terms. Robert Martin considers it to be 'largely a religious novel, concerned with the meaning of religion to man and its relevance to his behaviour'.[5] This, and the related moral issues, are so central to the presentation of Jane's experience that they require more extended discussion in the following chapter. Other critics relate these same moral issues to the theme of *human* rather than divine justice,[6] and this question too will be dealt with in what follows.

Some of the most challenging recent criticism, however, takes issue, by implication, with the concealed sexism of Martin's view – his use of the generic 'man' while discussing a novel by and about a woman. Feminist critics point out that the issues of both divine and human justice are presented through the more immediate and urgent problem of Jane's relationship with men. These issues are themselves seen in part as aspects of the patriarchal value system. We shall explore this view more fully in Chapter 7 of this *Guide*, which deals with recent critical approaches. In the meantime, what do *you* think are the main themes of *Jane Eyre*? What structures did you perceive in the text to suggest such a reading?

6. The Morality of the Novel

As I suggested at the end of the previous chapter, most critics would agree that morality is a principal theme in *Jane Eyre*, however much they might disagree as to whether this is presented in primarily religious terms, human terms, or in terms of sexual relationships. This chapter will, therefore, concentrate on the moral issues which appear to be so central to Jane's narrative. We need first to be clear that we are not looking for explicit moral statements representing the author's point of view: we cannot assume that the beliefs of the first-person narrator are those of the author, for even these may be qualified by the moral awareness expressed by the novel as a whole. Authors distance themselves from their narrators in varying degrees. But we shall also need, in concluding our discussion of these issues, to consider the whole notion of 'morality' in fiction – more specifically, to take account of the way in which this, like the related concept of 'realism', has been called into question by recent critical theory.

In *Jane Eyre*, moral issues are presented largely through an exploration of certain key concepts. Such concepts are tested, 'worked out', by being used in a variety of contexts. Their recurrence creates yet another pattern, another 'structure', drawing the reader's attention to the possibilities of meaning which accrue to the concept from each fresh context. There are many concepts we could usefully consider – 'obligation', 'power', 'conscience' and 'passion' are others you could work on for yourself – but I have picked out two which are central to the two dimensions of morality with which the novel is concerned. For morality is presented as an aspect both of human relationships, and of the relationship of the human to the non-human or divine.

The first of these concepts is 'obedience'. Look up the following examples of the word's use. What, if anything, do they have in common? Does Jane's view of what 'obedience' means, or entails, change? Or is it pretty consistent?

(1) 'Habitually *obedient* to John . . .' (Ch. I, p. 10)
(2) 'however carefully I *obeyed* . . .' (Ch. 4, p. 34)
(3) 'I was disposed to *obey* . . .' (Ch. 12, p. 116)
(4) 'We *obeyed*, as in duty bound . . .' (Ch. 13, p. 122)
(5) 'to *obey* you in all that is right . . .' (Ch. 20, p. 219)
(6) I was about mechanically to *obey* him . . .' (Ch. 24, p. 268)
(7) 'It would to *obey* you . . .' (Ch. 27, p. 320)
(8) 'I observed careful *obedience* . . .' (Ch. 34, p. 405)
(9) 'to coerce me into *obedience* . . .' (Ch. 34, p. 414)
(10) 'He *obeyed* at once . . .' (Ch. 35, p. 425)

DISCUSSION

In (1) to (4) obedience is instinctive for Jane. But in (1) she obeys only through fear, and in the second begins to question the value of unrewarded and unappreciated obedience, a view she continues to hold in spite of Helen Burns's example. Nevertheless, the habit of obedience remains, encouraged by Jane's sense of the obligations of the servant/master relationship – even when this involves leaving her bed in the middle of the night to tend a wounded man. (5), however, shows Jane challenging the virtues of unthinking obedience. The important qualification – 'in all that is right' – implies Jane's readiness to judge for herself what *is* right; it also implies that her master could conceivably ask her to do what was wrong. (6) illustrates this danger, and the ease with which she could drift into acquiescence, while (7) makes evident the possible conflict between obedience and duty.

St John Rivers, like Rochester, expects obedience from those around him, both as a man in an all-female household, and as a clergyman used to dictating the true way to his parishioners. Again Jane's habitual obedience makes her pliant to his requests for help in the school and with his desire to learn Hindostanee. But she is finally able to achieve command of herself: her freedom from the habit of acceptance is indicated by (10), one of the very rare occasions when the verb 'obeyed' is used of anyone other than Jane herself.

Rivers's justification for demanding obedience from Jane is that he is in fact demanding it for God: he calls himself 'the servant of an infallible master' (Ch. 34, p. 406). But the novel makes it clear that no human master – even the divinely inspired St John – is infallible. Jane must develop her own moral sense so that she can become, as she tells Rochester at the end of the novel, her own mistress. The master/servant image supports and amplifies the different implications of obedience. What Jane implicitly seeks is an equal relationship. Where conventional wisdom dictates that, in Mrs Fairfax's words 'Equality of position and fortune is often advisable in such cases' (Ch. 24, p. 267), Jane asserts the right to be considered as anyone's equal on moral grounds.

The word 'obedience' obviously occurs on many more occasions than we have time for here, and their effect in the course of reading is far richer and more subtle than my account can indicate. There is a gradual accumulation of meaning around this term and the concepts of master/servant and equality that relate to it. In arriving at a concept of obedience which rests ultimately on self-command and the individual conscience, Charlotte Brontë proposes a view of personal and social relationships which challenges every existing hierarchy – of sex and class – other than that of moral worth.[1]

Let us now look at the way the novel presents the relationship between the human and the non-human. 'It was my *nature* to feel pleasure in yielding to an authority supported like hers; and to bend, where my conscience and self-respect permitted, to an active will.' (Ch. 29, p. 348) In writing thus of her relationship with Diana Rivers, Jane asserts that, subject to those all-important qualifications, obedience is more *natural* to her than rebelliousness, provoked only by force of circumstance. The concept of 'nature' and what is 'natural' links Jane's individual moral development with the forces within and without her which determine that development. But the terms 'nature' and 'natural' are, of course, enormously complex and elusive. It would take too long to consider *all* the definitions listed by the Oxford English Dictionary, so I have made a selection of those which might be relevant to Jane's use of the term.

For 'nature':
- (i) A thing's essential qualities; person's innate character.
- (ii) Kind, sort, class.
- (iii) Inherent impulses determining character or action.
- (iv) Vital force or function or needs.
- (v) Physical power causing phenomena of the material world.

For 'natural':
- (vi) based on the *innate moral* sense, instinctive.
- (vii) constituted by nature.
- (viii) *normal*, conformable to the ordinary course of nature.
- (ix) *Not enlightened* or communicated by revelation.
- (x) Physically existing, not spiritual or intellectual or fictitious.
- (xi) Existing in or by nature, not *artificial*.

(My italics)

I'm sure you won't have needed my italics to draw your attention to the fact that many of these definitions are ideologically loaded – that is, they are based on assumptions and values which are not made explicit. They assume, for instance, a basic opposition between 'nature' and 'artifice', between the 'natural' and the 'abnormal', between the 'natural' and the 'spiritual'. And it would not be difficult, I think, to turn such oppositions on their head – to argue, for instance, that many physical 'abnormalities' occur 'naturally'. Furthermore, it does not take much thought to see that some of these definitions contradict others: 'natural' is 'moral' (vi), but also 'unenlightened' (ix). Finally, the implication that a 'moral sense' is 'instinctive' (vi) is one of the most important of those challenged by recent post-structuralist critics. However, we shall return to this issue later in the chapter. For the moment, having established the difficulties associated with the use of these terms, let us consider how they are used in *Jane Eyre*. Look up the following examples. Which of the given dictionary definitions apply to Jane's principal use or uses?

(1) 'It is as *natural* as that I should love those . . .' (Ch. 6, p. 58)
(2) 'the restlessness was in my *nature* . . .' (Ch. 12, p. 110)
(3) 'what I *naturally* and inevitably loved . . .' (Ch. 23, p. 254)
(4) '*Nature* meant me to be, on the whole, a good man . . .' (Ch. 14, p. 136)

(5) 'something lighter, franker, more *natural* as it were . . .' (Ch. 1, p. 7)
(6) 'it is no merit of yours: *Nature* did it . . .' (Ch. 14, p. 136)

(7) 'we are not to conform to *nature* . . .' (Ch. 7, p. 64)
(8) 'turn the bent of *nature* . . .' (Ch. 31, p. 366)
(9) 'But she could not eradicate *nature* . . .' (Ch. 32, p. 380)

DISCUSSION

In the first group of examples, Jane uses 'nature' in dictionary sense (i) or (iii), while Rochester uses the capitalized form to suggest something between (iv) and (v) – a 'power' or 'force' which determines not just the material world but the individual character. But it is also clear that Jane *justifies* her behaviour and feelings on the grounds that they are 'natural', implying dictionary definition (vi). Her rebelliousness, her restlessness, her love for Rochester, are all presented as 'natural'. But this is a dangerous form of defence, since, as we have seen from a brief examination of the recorded definitions, 'natural' can mean different things to different people, and can therefore be used to justify completely different standards. When Mrs Reed asks Jane to adopt a more 'natural' manner in (5), she is asking Jane to conform to her highly conventional expectations, to be 'normal' – OED definition (viii). In defending her restlessness in (2), however, Jane is opposing the reality of her individual self and experience *against* conventional expectations. Are we to accept Jane's defence that the 'natural' is desirable simply on the grounds that it is opposed to the conventional, or artificial – OED definition (xi)? In her Preface to the novel, Charlotte Brontë writes, 'Conventionality is not morality' (p. 3); but does the novel itself bear this out?

It is true that other characters appear to share Jane's view. Rochester claims his natural self is good, perverted only by circumstance (4). But he could, of course, be dismissed as the Devil's advocate. And he in a sense turns the tables on Jane by suggesting that, if Nature has made her what she is, she is neither culpable nor praiseworthy (6). It is ironic that he should echo the view of Helen Burns that there is no merit in passive goodness, only in constantly striving to cure one's faults, to combat one's nature (Ch. 6, p. 58). Quotations (7) to (9) express a view that contrasts totally with Jane's. The novel's clergymen, like Helen, insist that the individual must do constant battle with his or her nature in order to achieve Grace (OED definition ix). While the presentation of Mr Brocklehurst may prevent the reader from taking his views too seriously, Rivers presents more of a problem. Even if he is an unsuitable partner for Jane, may he not embody certain moral truths? Consider the following statements by St John. Compare them with (8) and (9) above. What do they indicate about his character and his morality?

(10) 'my *nature*, that God gave me . . .' (Ch. 30, p. 361)
(11) 'God and *nature* intended you for a missionary's wife.' (Ch. 34, p. 407)

DISCUSSION

These statements completely contradict the views expressed in (8) and (9). St John's inconsistency is symptomatic of the intense internal conflict under which he labours, and consequently undermines the authority of his judgments. Furthermore, while the 'natural' imagery – the imagery of the elements – emphasizes the dangerous power of the elements at work in the individual, it also suggests the need to recognize and give controlled expression to them. This imagery, relating the human to the non-human world, therefore reinforces Jane's view that what is 'natural' cannot and should not be totally denied.

One of Jane's implied criticisms of Rivers is that 'Nature was not to him that treasury of delight it was to his sisters' (Ch. 30, p. 356), whereas for Jane Nature is 'the universal mother' (Ch. 28, p. 327). I am suggesting that in *Jane Eyre* the concept of Nature or 'nature' is repeatedly associated with morally positive values. In this it demonstrates yet another aspect of its affinity with Romantic literature, particularly the poetry of Wordsworth. Wordsworth's *The Prelude* (1805) is probably the most fully developed literary exploration both of man's natural goodness, a belief inherited from Rousseau, and of Nature's role as inspiration, teacher and moral guide.

Here is an exercise for you to do by yourself. What meanings attach to the terms 'nature' and 'natural' in the following examples?

(1) 'now I was left in my *natural* element . . .' (Ch. 10, p. 85)
(2) 'I think you will learn to be *natural* with me . . .' (Ch. 14, p. 140)
(3) 'I must disown half my *nature* . . .' (Ch. 34, p. 403)
(4) 'What struggle there was in him between *Nature* and Grace . . .' (Ch. 35, p. 418)
(5) 'Insupportable – *unnatural* – out of the question!' (Ch. 35, p. 421)
(6) 'It brought to light and life my whole *nature* . . .' (Ch. 37, p. 442)

But is Nature presented as a religious force, as well as a moral one? The natural imagery is so closely related to the language and imagery of the Old Testament that it seems to refer the reader to an underlying theological framework. And when Jane experiences great deprivation after leaving Thornfield, it is Nature which sustains her – she senses God's presence in 'His works' (Ch. 28, pp. 328–9). But the relationship between nature and religion is more ambiguous than this might suggest, as Rivers's confused attitudes suggest.

One of the most problematic incidents in the novel occurs when Jane prays to Heaven to give her the right answer to St John's 'unnatural' proposal. In response she hears Rochester's voice calling to her. She calls this phenomenon 'the work of nature' (Ch. 35, p. 425). This might seem to indicate that the event is primarily a psychological one: Jane's own 'nature' is telling her what is right for her. But Rochester's story of having called out at the very same time that Jane heard his voice, and of having heard her voice in response, suggests something less easy to explain in rational terms. Are we perhaps dealing with a psychic phenomenon, an instance of extra-sensory perception occasioned by the intensity of feeling each has for the other? Or are we meant to fall back on a supernatural agency external to them both? If so, it would appear to confirm and sanction the desires of them both, the desires of their deeper natures. Neither Jane nor Rochester attempt to determine the exact source of this happening, and neither will I. You will, I am sure, have your own views.[2] But I do want to try to clarify the relationship between Nature and religion by considering more closely the role of religion in the novel.

The religious figures in the novel are not, as we have seen, presented in very positive terms. Even Helen Burns and Miss Temple are found wanting, while Brocklehurst represents all the most negative aspects of religion – punitive, frightening and repressive. Tom Winnifrith suggests this portrait openly expresses the contempt felt by all the Brontës for the extremes of Evangelicism and Calvinism.[3] While a belief in Heaven and Hell was shared by all Christians, only the Calvinists believed in a predetermined distinction between the elect and the damned, or used the prospect of eternal damnation as a means of inducing fear and obedience, as Brocklehurst does. Rejecting the fear of Hell as a motive for good, whether propounded by Brocklehurst or Rivers, Jane seeks and finds an ethical position based more on human need than on divine will, but she still appeals ultimately to a divine sanction for those needs.

Barry Qualls, however, views Jane's ethical position in very different terms, which conflict with my suggestion that the novel presents 'nature' as a force to be respected. He relates this aspect of the novel to a characteristic of Victorian novels in general. He sees there the convergence of two traditions – the seventeenth-century Puritan tradition of meditation upon the scriptures or upon men's lives as a means of edification, and the Romantic tradition which gave new, human-centred meanings to God and 'nature'. In his view, the Victorian novel shares the 'narrative linearity and the paradisal goal of the religious allegories', such as *Pilgrim's Progress*, searching for 'spiritual meaning behind the world of things', that is for 'natural supernaturalism'.[4]

Qualls points out the dangers, for Jane, in pursuing a human-centred morality. Her love for Rochester, for instance, temporarily blinds her to the promise of heavenly salvation, making her believe in the divinity of this life, tempting her into idolatry: 'He stood between me and every thought of religion . . . I could not, in those days, see God for his creature: of whom I had made an idol' (Ch. 24, p. 277). Qualls sees Jane as similarly being in danger of putting too much faith in nature: he suggests she learns that *denial* of the 'natural' self gives the soul greater power, and enables the individual to assert a self that encompasses an awareness of the non-self, the world beyond the self.

Critics in general seem divided between those who, like Qualls, see Jane's quest as one which ultimately has a religious focus and sanction, and those who see the religious imagery and language of the novel as metaphors for the over-riding priority of the *human* values represented.[5] We can try to evaluate these alternatives by again considering the novel's ending. Qualls believes that Charlotte Brontë uses Jane's marriage and Rivers' self-denying mission as alternative forms of the 'New Jerusalem'.

Jane's achievement is as fully a religious one as Rivers, if not more so, since his action 'is a denial of the godborn in man, of that which requires him to live amongst his fellows with responsibility for them'.[6] Read the last chapter of the novel in the light of Qualls's argument. Is Jane's marriage presented as a means of religious fulfilment? Or does it represent an *alternative* to traditional Christian values and goals? Why do you think that the novel ends with St John's anticipated death rather than with Jane's own wedded bliss? What light does this sombre conclusion throw on their union? Examine, in particular, the language of Jane's eulogy of St John (pp. 457–8). What is the significance of such phrases as 'ambition', 'first rank', 'master-spirit', and 'who are called, and chosen, and faithful'? Is there anything distinctive about the syntax? And who, or what, is the main grammatical subject? You may find it helpful to refer back to the linguistic analysis we carried out in Chapter 3 of this *Guide* (pp. 32–8).

DISCUSSION

On hearing of Jane's marriage, St John warns Jane against living only for earthly things, a reminder of her earlier 'idolatry'. Jane's first reference to her marriage might suggest his fears are justified: 'I know what it is to live entirely for and with what I love best on earth' (p. 456). In contrast, St John's life is presented as that of an indefatigable saver of souls. The final paragraph on p. 457 has many of the 'poetic' qualities we have seen to be characteristic of Charlotte Brontë's prose – imagery, allusions, syntactic inversions – and the paratactic constructions, such as 'he labours for his race: he clears their painful way to improvement; he hews down like a giant . . .', underline the effect of intense and continuous energy generated by the vocabulary. But the passage also has the characteristics of public, rather than personal, utterance. The repetition, the accumulated adjectives, and the superlative statement – 'A more resolute, indefatigable pioneer never wrought amidst rocks and dangers' – make it extremely rhetorical.

This rhetorical effect reaches a climax in the ostentatious syntactic structure of the second half of the paragraph: the thrice-repeated 'He may be . . .' leads into a trio of clauses of parallel construction – 'his is the . . . who . . .'. The rather unusual construction, 'His is the sternness . . .', rather than 'his sternness is . . .', ensures the rhythmic emphasis falls on 'his', as it earlier fell on 'he', and echoes such familiar biblical phrasing as 'Thine is the kingdom . . .'. 'He', St John, is the subject of every sentence, so that the sheer weight of 'he' and 'his' throughout the passage conveys the impression of a powerful and single-minded individual. Assertion follows assertion in what appears to be a whole-hearted affirmation of St John's achievement.

And yet, isn't the final effect rather different? Did you feel, as I did, that Jane overstates her case? And where *is* Jane? I have found very few other paragraphs in the novel – and none of this length – where the narrator is totally absent, where there is no 'I', or 'me' or 'my'. The only hint of a *personal* attitude to the statements being enunciated is in the modal verb 'may' in 'He *may* be stern . . .', but this qualification is immediately countered by the following images and allusions which give St John an appropriately saint-like status. You may want to argue that Jane's personal view is expressed in the affirmations of the eulogy themselves, and do not require any additional validation. But to me this almost unique degree of self-effacement on Jane's part suggests private – perhaps unconscious – reservations beneath this very 'public' homage. Is this perhaps a case of very subtle self-deception?

Even if we disregard these possible reservations, there remains the implied egoism of 'ambition', 'first rank', and 'master-spirit', and what I regard as the very significant echoes in the final clauses of this paragraph: 'who share the last mighty victories of the lamb; who are called, and chosen, and faithful'. For Jane, too, is often likened by Rochester to a lamb; she too is 'called' by an inexplicable voice, 'chosen' ('Choose, then, sir – *her who loves you best*' (Ch. 37, p. 450)) and 'faithful' ('I am still his right hand' (p. 456)). Even St John's final words are an echo of Jane's on hearing Rochester's voice. Are we to regard this as simply further evidence of idolatry? I think not, if we remember the precedents of biblical and religious literature: Eve was made of Adam's rib, just as Jane is 'bone of his bone'. If we accept Rochester's Christian repentance as complete, then the union can be seen in the Miltonic terms of *Paradise Lost* – 'He for God only, she for God in him' (Book IV, l. 299).

I would agree, then, with Qualls's assertion that Jane's marriage is presented as an alternative means of fulfilling one's 'mission', of living the true Christian life. Unlike Qualls, however, I do not see this religious goal as one that repudiates the 'natural', since it is 'nature' that has called Jane back to Rochester and marriage. The 'natural' and human are endowed with the sanctity of the divine. The tension between 'human tears' and 'Divine joy' with which the novel ends suggests an ability to partake in both the sacred and the profane which is arguably Jane's major achievement.

Nevertheless, the comparison between these two contrasted modes of fulfilment is seen in a very different light by Annette Tromly, who rejects the 'Paradisal' interpretation of the novel's ending.[7] She suggests that Jane is inspired by Rivers's mission and the absolute certainty he feels about the rightness of his choice – inspired to a kind of envy of his heroic destiny, compared with her humdrum everyday existence at Ferndean. How fair a reading of Jane's reactions do you think this is? Very? Plausible, but not entirely convincing? Quite wrong?

I am not myself convinced that certainty of this kind is what Jane seeks. Has not such certainty been presented again and again as suspect, often allied to inhuman dogma? Remember Brocklehurst, Rivers, and even Helen Burns or again Rochester (in certain respects) – all found wanting because of their stubborn conviction that *they* know what is right for others. In sharp contrast, Jane's readiness to question, and to remain open to new possibilities, is what enables her to grow emotionally and spiritually. My own response to Jane's eulogy of Rivers is, as I have indicated, that it is an overt expression of certainty undercut by the narrator's self-suppression. Whether the narrator *herself* is lulled into complacency by the 'certainty' of her love for Rochester is a question we shall return to in the following chapter.

I have been arguing that *Jane Eyre* presents 'nature' as a moral force to be listened to with respect. But we should not simply accept this, or any other moral concept embodied in the novel as a universal 'truth'. As I said at the beginning of this chapter, recent criticism has challenged the traditional view that fiction embodies moral 'truths', stressing instead that fiction is a form of *ideology* – it embodies values and beliefs which are intimately related to the existing social and political system. Whereas the OED definition of 'natural' as 'based on the innate moral sense; instinctive' implies that morality *is* 'innate', Roland Barthes argues that the so-called 'morality' of the novel is no more than an arrangement of concepts, presented through received language and cultural and literary codes, which we have been *taught* to perceive as 'moral'. The weight of received ideas in the text, ideas which we grow up accepting as 'general knowledge' or 'common sense', ensures that the values of a particular culture are passed off as 'universal moral truths'.[8] We have seen these received ideas in operation in the dictionary definitions of 'natural', which refer to oppositions and associations embedded in our language system, itself a manifestation of a particular culture.

We need, therefore, to be aware that, while Jane Eyre *appears* to challenge and question conventional moral and social standards, that very challenge rests on values and assumptions not made explicit in the text. While she *appears* to be a rigorous searcher for truth, sincere and consistent, she is not always aware of the implications of her own behaviour and feelings. Both her eulogy of St John and the contradictory structures perceptible in the novel suggest to me that her questioning may be constrained by her acceptance of certain moral concepts as absolute.

Let us take, as a further example, the ambiguity which some hostile critics have seen in Jane's attitude towards Rochester, and her own sexuality. D. H. Lawrence attacked the novel in these terms:

> I find *Jane Eyre* verging towards pornography . . . the strongest instincts have collapsed, and sex has become something slightly

> obscene, to be wallowed in, but despised. Mr Rochester's sex passion is not 'respectable' till Mr Rochester is burned, blinded, disfigured, and reduced to helpless dependence. Then, thoroughly humbled and humiliated, it may be merely admitted.[9]

Lawrence's argument implies that the existence of Rochester's first wife is not the only – or even the most important – reason for Jane leaving him: although she does not acknowledge it, his sexuality is what drives Jane away. *Is* Jane deceiving herself about her motives at this point? Is she sufficiently *aware* of her feelings about Rochester, or of her *own* sexuality? In Ch. 27 (pp. 305–11), Jane and Rochester discuss Bertha's insanity. Do they indicate any cause for it? How do the attitudes that emerge from this discussion compare with the view of womanhood suggested by the following quotations? Are Jane's views on these two occasions consistent?

(1) 'Jane Eyre, who had been an ardent, expectant *woman* – almost a bride – was a cold, solitary *girl* again.' (Ch. 26, p. 298)
(2) 'How can I, a man not yet thirty, take out with me to India a *girl* of nineteen, unless she be married to me? . . . you have a *woman*'s heart, and – it would not do.' (Ch. 34, p. 413)
(3) 'I have a *woman*'s heart; but not where you are concerned.' (Ch. 34, p. 413)

(My italics)

DISCUSSION

Rochester presents Bertha's insanity as hereditary, but 'her excesses had prematurely developed the germs of insanity (p. 311): she was 'at once intemperate and unchaste' (p. 310). The association between female sexuality and madness is traditional, and I want to return to the role of Bertha in the following chapter. For the moment, let us just note that to emphasize what it is that alienates him from his wife, Rochester asserts 'it is not because she is mad I hate her' (p. 305), and swears he would continue to love *Jane* if she went mad. Isn't the implication here that in Jane insanity could *not* be the result of sexual excess? Doesn't it further imply an ambiguity in Rochester's attitude, since he is appalled by his wife's intemperance, but wishes to make Jane his mistress?

As for the quotations, (1) contrasts 'girl' and 'woman' in terms which imply not only a contrast between virginity and sexual experience, but a very positive view of sexual experience. To be a 'woman', it is implied, is to be sexually fulfilled. Similarly, doesn't Rivers imply – and Jane confirm – in (2) that, although only nineteen,

Jane has the feelings, sexual feelings, of a mature woman? The horror of sexuality suggested by the sex/madness association is, therefore, contrasted with these tacit reminders of Jane's 'passionate' nature, that word 'ardent' connecting with the fire imagery which reflects that nature. These contradictions and inconsistencies inevitably enter into Jane's presentation of her love for Rochester. She appeared ready to accept him as he was *before* she found out about Bertha; why, then, does he have to undergo such dramatic changes? The traditional answer has been that these changes demonstrate a moral growth which makes him a more appropriate partner for the heroine, and (as I have suggested) there is also a significant role reversal which makes him less of a threat to Jane's integrity (see Chapter 4 of this *Guide*). But the problems we have just discussed suggest a confusion in Jane about her own and Rochester's sexuality which makes Lawrence's charge that the ending represents a sexual taming, a symbolic castration, worth taking seriously.

In fact, rather than seeing this in terms of 'moral growth', it may be more accurate to see it as an illustration of the process of *internalization* – the process by which an individual makes a principle or value a conscious or unconscious part of the self, as the result of learning or repeated social experiences. From this point of view, Jane learns – through punishment (in the Red Room), rejection (being sent to Lowood), and reward (in the form of the affection of Helen and Miss Temple) – that uncontrolled passionate feeling is unacceptable in young women, and must be held in check by what are called 'duty' and 'conscience' – an internalized form of repression. The novel's conclusion, therefore, demonstrates not the triumph of the individual moral sense, but the triumph of the dominant ideology, as it relates to the question of what is 'womanly' and what is 'moral'.

This process, by which human subjects submit themselves to a dominant ideology, has been related by some theorists to the acquisition of language.[10] Language, as we saw in the previous chapter, is a system which generates meaning through differences. Born into this system, the human subject acquires a sense of identity and definition through a growing awareness, fostered by that system, of everything that identifies that subject in terms of what he or she is *not*. The subject's sense of social identity, which makes the individual feel *part* of this symbolic order of language, rests therefore on this sense of *difference*, most obviously of sexual and social difference. But since language is a system outside the individual's control, the identity fostered by that system is always going to be at best an approximation, at worst a misnomer. So Jane Eyre, at the beginning of the novel, is labelled, differentiated, as unacceptably passionate and of inferior status – 'you are less than a servant . . . you are under obligation' (Ch. 2, p. 12). Brocklehurst, representing authority, explicitly labels Jane 'a liar'. Being thus differentiated, Jane ultimately accepts such distinctions, as her later preoccupation with her own social status (self-consciously a 'lady' even when a beggar), and the need to submit passion to 'duty' indicate. That is, Jane can be seen as spending the whole of her adult life trying to be what, in childhood, she was defined as *not* being – hence the sense of conflicting and contradictory forces at work in the novel. The structure of binary opposites (see Chapter 5 of this *Guide*, pp. 57–8) represents this struggle, which ultimately results in social conformity. Jane's readiness, in the final chapter, to 'name', to define, all those around her with an unquestioning assertiveness is evidence, according to this reading, of how totally she has been absorbed into the social order represented by the language system.[11]

These different critical perspectives clearly raise important questions as regards such concepts as 'nature' and 'morality'. The following chapter includes discussion of Marxist and feminist readings of the novel which explicitly take issue with the social and sexual 'differences' presented in the novel as 'natural'.

7 Recent Critical Approaches

This guide to recent criticism is necessarily selective. I have selected both the most interesting and challenging criticism of *Jane Eyre*, and those works of critical theory which you need to consider if you are attempting a serious study of any novel. If you want to know how these selected views relate to current trends in general, the 'Further

Reading' list includes a number of sources which provide a good overall view.

Having considered the novel as a whole, and some mainline views of it, you can now approach some more recent discussion in an appropriately critical frame of mind, testing its usefulness against your own developed sense of the work.

Structuralist criticism

We can begin with structuralist criticism, since we have already discussed the main principles of structural linguistics on which it is based (see pp. 62). To review that earlier discussion, meaning is not inherent in the individual word, but derives from that word's *syntagmatic* and *paradigmatic* relationships – its relationship to the other words in the sentence and to every other word in the 'paradigm' or grammatical set to which it belongs. Similarly, structuralist literary criticism considers the meaning of a text to lie in the relationship between its different elements. While this in itself may not sound a very revolutionary idea, what is specific to the structuralist emphasis is the exclusion of any reference to what lies outside the text for an explanation of its meaning: it is 'immanent' criticism. The text is no longer seen as being a representation of the real world, or even as an expression of the writer's feelings about it, but as a linguistic structure. Structuralist critics are less concerned with *what* a text means, than *how* it means. They have, in general, shown less interest in the individuality of a text than in examining it as an example of the way the literary system operates, drawing attention to the amount of commonplace stock material which every literary work employs.

But the term 'structuralist' covers many different critics, with many different emphases.[1] One branch of structuralism specifically relevant to novel criticism is 'narratology', which looks for the basic, recurrent structures in all narratives. This subject is particularly relevant to a novel which purports to be a narrative constructed by its own central character. One of the most thorough analysts of narrative is Gerard Genette. His book, *Narrative Discourse,*[2] at first sight appears intimidating, both because of its unfamiliar terminology and because of its use of Marcel Proust's *À la Recherche du temps perdu* as its sole text for reference. However, if you approach this book slowly and patiently, I think you will find it surprisingly comprehensible. The book's primary aim is to study the relationship between 'discourse' (the written text), 'story' (the events recounted), and 'narrating' (the act of telling the story). Using the linguistic model as the basis for his analysis, Genette draws an analogy between the sentence and the narrative text, treating narrative as 'the expansion of a verb', analysed according to the three categories of 'tense', 'mood', and 'voice'. I want to suggest how one of the more straightforward aspects of tense – duration – can be applied to *Jane Eyre*. This will, I hope, help you to approach the rest of this fascinating book for yourself.

Genette begins by pointing out that we cannot measure the duration of the discourse, the text, since every reader will experience it differently, according to reading speed, the circumstances in which the text is read, and so on. What we can measure, however, is the 'steadiness of speed' – the relationship between the duration of the story (in days, months or years) and the length of text allocated to each fictional period (measured in lines or pages). A novel which devoted one page to each fictional day would have 'isochrony' – unchanging speed. But in practice changes in speed, or 'anisochronies', provide the novel's essential rhythm. Usually, for instance, there is a slowing down of the narrative in scenes of importance, while a period considered insignificant in terms of the narrative is represented by an ellipsis, which indicates the passing of time without indicating what took place during that time. Genette suggests there are four basic forms of narrative movement – ellipsis, pause, scene and summary. In an ellipsis, narrative time – the time taken to recount events – is infinitely less than story time, while in a pause it is infinitely greater, as the story proper is brought to a halt to allow for description. In a scene, particularly one consisting largely of dialogue, narrative time and story time are conventionally equal, while in summary narrative time is again less than story time.

To assess the relevance of these categories to *Jane Eyre*, you could find examples of each of these narrative movements, and so chart the rhythm of the novel, its climaxes and lulls, the sense of time passing and so on. As a means of assessing your grasp of the difference between these 'movements', you might like to decide how you would label the beginning of Ch. 10 (pp. 83–4). Is it a summary, or an ellipsis? Jane writes, 'I now pass a space of eight years almost in silence', which would seem to indicate an ellipsis, but notice that she does give us *some* information. Genette notes that, until the twentieth century, summary was the usual means of transition between scenes in fiction, a kind of connective tissue in the fundamental rhythm of scene and summary. An ellipsis, on the other hand, indicates the lapse of time between scenes with *minimal* 'diegetic' content, that is, with the minimum of descriptive comment by the narrator, as in 'some years *of happiness* passed'. Occasionally, in an *implicit* ellipsis, the reader has to infer the passage of time from a gap in the narrative continuity. This is clearly not the case in our example from *Jane Eyre*, nor can the diegetic content be classed as minimal, so that we appear to be dealing with the more traditional summary.

However, Genette's application of these categories to Proust's work suggests that, as with so much structuralist criticism, the most interesting results come from an examination of those points at which the novel departs from the norm, or pushes it to the limit. He suggests, for instance, that there are few true 'pauses' in Proust's work, few moments when the narrator provides descriptive material solely to provide the reader with information about a character or place. Proust's descriptions never suspend the story because they are, in fact, part of the action, which Genette describes as 'a narrative and analysis of the perceptual activity of the character contemplating'.[3] Does this comment seem relevant to *Jane Eyre*?

You may feel that the action of *Jane Eyre* consists of the events on which she, as an adult, is looking back. At one level this is clearly true, and such descriptions as occur could be said to indicate a break in these events. But if you look, for instance, at Jane's description of the parlour of Moor House and its inhabitant, St John Rivers, in Ch. 29 (p. 349), then this 'pause' clearly represents the activity of contemplation which Jane undertook at the time. If we turn to Jane's description of John Reed in Ch. 1 (p. 10), this is closer to a 'true pause', in so far as it conveys information known to Jane over a long period, and imparted here purely for the convenience of the reader. Nevertheless, it seems to me arguable that the 'action' of *Jane Eyre*, a novel in which the presence of the narrator is so strongly felt, could be seen as the process of looking back and recalling, or re-creating, her life. If the novel is seen in these terms, then Genette's comments on the absence of the true pause in Proust's work perhaps provides another explanation for the constant sense of 'activity' in *Jane Eyre*, even when the narrated Jane is physically inactive and alone.

One critic who does see *Jane Eyre* as 'a narrative and analysis of the perceptual activity of the character contemplating', to use Genette's phrase, is Annette Tromly. Her book, *The Cover of the Mask*,[4] shows the influence of structuralist criticism in that it sees the text as being 'about' its own process of construction, rather than the 'reality' of Jane's former experiences. She suggests that Charlotte Brontë uses the autobiographical form to explore 'the motives, principles and practices of self-presentation' (p. 14); and that the novelist recognizes that autobiography necessarily distorts the truth, because of its subjectivity. Moreover Brontë's autobiographers are all, in some respect, artists, so that their narrative function is riddled with ambiguity: on the one hand is the commitment to tell the truth, on the other the artist's desire to shape the raw material of life into art.

Tromly suggests, therefore, that Charlotte Brontë's novels invite us to see the narrators quite differently from the way they see themselves; they require us to be ready to discern the possibility of self-deception in these autobiographies:

> Brontë's narrators create personal mythologies about themselves, mythologies which in their view endow their lives with heightened moral significance. In their accounts of their past – of the choices they made, the priorities they established, the wrongs they perceived – they often present to us, to use Charlotte's terms, 'pattern [s] of perfection', with all the blots veiled. In claiming this heightened moral significance, the narrators elevate their quotidian pursuits; they present themselves as prototypes for the revelation of human meaning. (p. 15)

Such an approach requires us above all to consider the narrative as Jane's, rather than the author's. That is, we have to see the methods Brontë employs as being chosen as much for what they indicate about Jane herself, as for what they indicate about the situations and characters depicted. For instance, the symbolic use of physical description, which we discussed in Chapter 3 of this *Guide* is perceived by Annette Tromly as evidence of Jane's tendency to romanticize, her tendency to continually transform the concrete into the symbolic, to perceive everything in terms of its significance for herself, rather than in its own right. I am not myself convinced that Jane is such a romanticizer as this, as my discussion in Chapter 4 will have indicated. Nevertheless, the idea that we need to adopt a critical position towards the narrator, rather than identifying her too closely with the author, merits serious consideration.

In the first chapter of this *Guide* we considered the way that the adult narrator's comments call into question the reliability of the child's perceptions. How are we to judge whether that adult narrator is herself unreliable? Obviously any autobiographical account will be subjective, but against what can we measure its distortions? The dialogue and 'showings' of the novel are conventionally assumed to provide some kind of objective evidence against which to measure the narrator's 'tellings' (see p. 11). If they are *not* evidence of external 'reality', but simply another aspect of Jane's *construction* of reality, then what means do we have of checking the narrator's truthfulness or power of judgment? Can Tromly's thesis, interesting as a hypothesis, be borne out by the evidence of the text?

Tromly herself suggests this unreliability is indicated by what she calls 'leakages': referring to the 'patterns of moral progress' which Brontë's autobiographers create for themselves, she writes:

> All three personal mythologies reflect a pronounced constriction of outlook, a chosen containment by the autobiographer of what is irreducible in his life to the terms of a paradigm. Inevitably, these paradigms suffer from 'leakage'. Presenting neatly finished portraits of themselves in the novels, the narrators are betrayed by the loose ends which Brontë dangles before the reader. (p. 16)

As a possible example of such a 'leakage', I want you to consider Jane's account of what happened to Adèle. Please re-read pp. 455 to 456 (Ch. 38). What are your reactions to Jane's treatment of Adèle? How does it compare with Mrs Reed's treatment of Jane at the beginning of the novel?

DISCUSSION

There is clearly no question of physical or mental cruelty here, and Jane deliberately withdraws Adèle from the school where she is unhappy, in contrast to Mrs Reed's total lack of interest in Jane's welfare at Lowood. Nevertheless, is there not something discordant, an implied restriction of feeling and concern, about Jane's abandonment of her plans to become the child's governess, because her 'times and cares were now required by another' – Rochester? I am inclined to agree with Annette Tromly's reading here:

> Although she seems to have become the model child that Jane never could be, Adèle is nevertheless being judged by the same cold standards:
>
> > As she grew up, a sound, English education corrected in a great measure her French defects; and when she left school, I found in her a pleasing and obliging companion: docile, good-tempered and well-principled. By her grateful attention to me and mine, she has long since well repaid any little kindness I ever had it in my power to offer her. (576)
>
> Jane's self-satisfied condescension to the child echoes the bloodless attitude of her own first guardian; in becoming Mrs Rochester, she has somehow dissolved into Mrs Reed. Adèle's unfortunate situation delicately insinuates itself into Jane's happy ending. (p. 60)

If Jane's treatment of Adèle thus casts doubt on the validity of Jane's total absorption in Rochester, then it confirms the possibility that the novel's ending as a whole, usually taken as Charlotte Brontë's resolution, is only Jane's. That is, what we may first interpret as a convincing moral ideal is to be challenged and questioned.

I have already discussed Tromly's uneasiness about the novel's 'happy ending' in Chapter 6 of this *Guide*, so I will give you just one final comment for consideration:

> The sense of satisfying closure which Jane claims in her autobiography's final chapters, then, is qualified by the reader's sense of her claustrophobia. For rather than beginning her life at Ferndean, she seems to be living her death instead. Nothing remains for her to do with herself. She can only revitalize a static life by writing it; she can only attempt a resurrection by turning to autobiography. (p. 61)

Ultimately this critic sees the very activity of autobiography as a self-limiting act: 'in defining themselves, they confine themselves.' (p. 18) You might like to compare this view with that expressed by Tony Tanner, who suggests this process of self-definition is a positive, creative act for a woman otherwise deprived of identity in an indifferent society. He sees the novel as being primarily about the creation of a self out of language: Jane's development is a process of learning to say, 'I am', to assert her own identity on her own terms. It is also a process of learning to define those around her in such a way as to understand and thus control the threat they represent to her sense of self. The narrator, who is of course at the end of that learning process, uses the verbal form of the narrative to give shape and meaning to her experience.[5]

My own view, as I have already indicated, is that the limited future envisioned for Jane at the end of the novel is a comment on the position of women at that time. *Approval* of this ending is not necessarily implied by its mere existence, nor does the marriage totally undermine Jane's achievement, however limited. Tanner's reading is, in this respect, a fair one, although it fails to engage with the possibility that Jane's 'control' is ultimately excessive. However, the value of Tromly's approach, like Tanner's, is that it alerts us to the possibilities of falsification and myth-making inherent in the narrative act itself. By drawing attention to the process of construction, it prevents us from assuming a direct, unproblematic relationship between author and narrator, between narrator and the narrated Jane, and between the tale and the experiences it purports to re-enact.

Post-structuralism

Post-structuralism goes beyond structuralism in a number of ways. Rather than simply demonstrating the structures through which a text has meaning, post-structuralist critics attempt to analyse the significance – ideological or psychological – of those structures. This means the 'immanent' approach has to be abandoned, since such an analysis requires consideration not only of the codes and conventions of the literary system, but of those of the society to which those literary codes are related. Roland Barthes' 'semic code', for instance, can only be understood in terms of the stereotypes and conventions of the culture within which this literary code is used (see Chapter 2 of this *Guide*, pp. 18–19).

Barthes' *S/Z* is one of the most important examples of post-structuralist criticism, since it represents a fundamental challenge to the traditional concept of realism.[6] It examines the structures and codes of nineteenth-century realism through a phrase-by-phrase, even word-by-word analysis of a short story by Balzac. In this work Barthes demonstrates how the text uses 'signs', codified indications of a reality which the reader is assumed to share. The reader interprets these signs, not by measuring the 'reality' of the novel against the 'reality' of the world, since neither reader nor writer perceives 'reality' directly. That perception is mediated and codified, a pattern being imposed upon it by their ideological situation. Instead, the reader interprets one code in terms of another – the literary in terms of the cultural.

Barthes suggests that the classic realist text operates according to five 'codes'. To the 'hermeneutic' code belong all those textual units whose function is to articulate a question and its answer, as well as the many elements which define the nature of the question, or problem, or delay its solution. The most obvious enigma element in *Jane Eyre* is provided by reference to the woman in the attic. As we read, we attempt to answer the questions raised by this mysterious presence. The second 'proairetic' code, the code of actions, implies a logic in human behaviour which enables the reader to determine the result of an action. That is, we expect any action depicted in a novel to indicate a specific intention on the part of an actor: action in fiction is not random and arbitrary, but always indicative. Even the most apparently insignificant act is read as an indication of a purpose or cause. We similarly can expect the completion of an action to have specific consequences. This does not mean that all elements of surprise or unpredictability are removed, but that they can only function against a background of expectation. We have already discussed the 'semic' code, the code of character and theme, in Chapter 2 of this *Guide*, and we have had plenty of opportunity to see the 'symbolic' code at work in *Jane Eyre*, the code which enables the reader to interpret a detail or event as having more than its literal meaning.

Arguably the most important of all the codes is the 'cultural or reference' code. This includes all those references to norms by which we interpret action: in our culture, for instance, a slammed door indicates anger, a wrinkled brow thought and so on. This body of 'common sense', of 'general knowledge', to which the text continually refers, provides a framework of scientific and moral 'authority' which the novelist uses to validate his or her point of view. It contains all the stereotypes and clichés of a culture. 'If we collect all such knowledge, all such vulgarisms, we create a monster, and this monster is ideology. As a fragment of ideology, the cultural code inverts its class origin (scholastic and social) into a natural reference, into a proverbial statement.' (p. 97).

These codes combine together to create the illusion of reality. 'Reality' or 'life' in the classic realist text is, therefore, 'a smothering layer of received ideas' (p. 206). But these class-based ideas and prejudices are transformed into a point of reference which the reader accepts as 'real', 'normal', 'natural', in the process known as 'naturalization'.[7] As an expression of the naturalizing process in literature, realism is thus seen by critics like Barthes as having an ideological function, attempting to pass off as 'real', as inevitably and indubitably there, that which is temporary and man-made. For it is the function of ideology to 'naturalize' social reality, to make the existing social structure seem eternal and universal, an expression of the 'natural' order.

One of the most important aspects of post-structuralism, therefore, is the process known as 'deconstruction'.[8] The originator of this concept, the French philosopher, Jacques Derrida, suggests that what are often considered to be the 'first principles' on which a social or philosophical system is based, its very foundation, are merely the product of that system, an attempt to justify it – an ideology. His interest in any text, therefore, lies in 'de-constructing' those first principles. To deconstruct a text is to analyse its internal contradictions and discontinuities, its implicit omissions, in such a way as to expose the weaknesses and contradictions within its ruling ideology – the structure of ideas which constitute both its vision of the world and a system of values. In so doing, deconstruction can expose the real power structure which that ideology attempts to justify. Literary critics who have been influenced by Derrida put great stress, furthermore, on the sense in which texts always undercut and subvert their *own* efforts at coherence and clarity.

Annette Tromly's discussion of the 'leakages' in Jane's narrative pattern could be seen as an example of deconstruction, but in concentrating on the narrator's text, rather than the author's, she does not really pursue the ideological implications of the text. In considering Jane's final comments on Adèle, for instance, she does not seem to consider whether they may be as much a measure of Charlotte Brontë's chauvinism as of Jane's limitations.

The term 'natural' is used throughout the novel as a measure of value, as the exercise we carried out in the previous chapter indicated. What implicit, assumed values and social prejudices does this conceal? Make notes on this subject before you move on to the following pages which deal with critical approaches closely allied to post-structuralism in their emphasis on the ideology of the text.

Feminist criticism

Feminist criticism focuses on the sexual ideology of the text, attempting in particular to undermine the binary oppositions between male and female on which the patriarchal vision of so much nineteenth-century fiction is based.

In their study of women's writing from Jane Austen onwards, Sandra Gilbert and Susan Gubar analyse the recurrent themes and imagery. They note the pervasive images of enclosure, indications that these women were

> literally and figuratively confined. Enclosed in the architecture of an overwhelmingly male-dominated society, these literary women were also, inevitably, trapped in the specifically *literary* constructs of what Gertrude Stein was to call 'patriarchal poetry'.[9]

Women writers, they suggest, have to examine and transcend these literary constructs if they are to transform oppressive conventions; specifically, they have to deal with those oppositions between 'angel' and 'monster' which seem to represent male ambivalence towards women, and particularly towards their sexuality.

But the authors make it clear that 'monsters' are not only to be found in male writing. The tradition of uncontrollable madness, often associated with sexuality, is common in female literature too. And even those women writers wishing to resist this internalization of patriarchal structures often do so indirectly, through surface plots which appear to conform, while concealing deeper, less acceptable levels of meaning which subvert those structures. Gilbert and Gubar suggest that the 'concealed plot' in most nineteenth-century women's writing is the quest for self-definition. Within this plot, melodramatic characters such as Bertha Mason act out the subversive impulses of women who appear to accept the evils of patriarchy.

Sandra Gilbert's analysis of *Jane Eyre* concentrates on the confrontation with Bertha, an encounter for Jane 'not with her own sexuality but with her own imprisoned "hunger, rebellion and rage"' (p. 339) for Bertha is

> Jane's truest and darkest double: she is the angry aspect of the orphan child, the ferocious secret self Jane has been trying to repress ever since her days at Gateshead . . . Specifically, every one of Bertha's appearances – or, more accurately, her manifestations – has been associated with an experience (or repression) of anger on Jane's part. (p. 360)[10]

In contrast, figures like Miss Temple represent the repression of that anger, teaching Jane survival through apparent conformity.

According to this reading, what Jane is looking for in her relationship with Rochester is an equality which will obviate the need for anger and rebellion. But she is uncertain whether this is to be found in marriage:

> Though she loves Rochester the man, Jane has doubts about Rochester the husband even before she learns about Bertha. In her world, she senses, even the equality of love between true minds leads to the inequalities and minor despotisms of marriage. 'For a little while,' she says cynically to Rochester, 'you will perhaps be as you are now, [but] . . . I suppose your love will effervesce in six months, or less. I have observed in books written by men, that period assigned as the farthest to which a husband's ardor extends' (Chapter 24) . . . And that hostility becomes overt at the silk warehouse, where Jane notes that 'the more he bought me, the more my cheek burned with a sense of annoyance and degradation'. (pp. 356–7)

But by the end of the novel the situation has changed considerably. As Bertha herself dies in the flames, so the Bertha in Jane dies when she is freed, by Rochester's call, from life-long subjugation to Rivers. For the impediments to equality between Jane and Rochester have been removed with the casting off of those 'social disguises – master/servant, prince/Cinderella' (p. 368), which perpetuate inequality. Rochester's blinding is thus a traditional symbol of his newfound clarity of perception.

Gilbert accepts that the ending of the novel appears to represent a withdrawal, emphasizing the couple's 'spiritual isolation in a world where such egalitarian marriages as theirs are rare, if not impossible' (p. 369). She suggests Charlotte Brontë was only 'able to act out that passionate drive towards freedom which offended agents of the status quo', not 'consciously to define the full meaning of achieved freedom'; this critic nevertheless believes that the novelist makes clear the value of Jane's achievement as opposed to St John's. She believes the novel was written to repudiate such a denial of self as he proposes for others and accepts for himself:

> As for the Celestial City itself, Charlotte Brontë implies here . . . that such a goal is the dream of those who accept inequities on earth, one of the many tools used by patriarchal society to keep, say, governesses in their 'place'. (p. 370)

You will have to decide for yourself whether you share this view of the novel's ending, or that of critics like Annette Tromly, who see the marriage as belonging to what Gilbert and Gubar term the 'surface plot', the conformist element. You should note, however, that both these critical works read the novel as a feminist text. But while Gilbert and Gubar read Charlotte Brontë's feminism in the nature of the ending itself, Tromly sees it only in her questioning of that ending. As far as the analysis of Bertha's significance is concerned, I find *The Madwoman in the Attic* very persuasive, although I feel that the authors exaggerate the extent of Jane's submissiveness, in order to emphasize the distinction between 'surface' and 'concealed' plots. Jane's readiness to defend Bertha from Rochester's abuse, to suggest that she is not to blame for being as she is, seems to me to substantiate the idea that Jane recognizes an identity with Bertha. They share not only their anger but their vulnerability: Jane, too, has been locked away, and dismissed from respectable family life because of her irrationality and her anger.

In conclusion you should consider for yourself what comment the novel has to make on the notion of what is 'womanly': what light does Jane's own refusal to conform, and her insistence that women have as much need as men to be active (Ch. 12, p. 110), throw on this subject? What comment do you feel the novel makes on the power structure latent in male–female relationships?

Marxist criticism

Terry Eagleton's study of the Brontë novels, *Myths of Power*,[11] adopts an explicitly Marxist viewpoint which takes into account these sexual issues as well as the social issues involved, recognizing that they are indeed difficult to separate. His analysis of the relevance of the biographical and social background of the Brontës is far more subtle and complex than the simple matching of fiction to fact about which I have already expressed reservations. In his Introduction, Eagleton defines the aim of Marxist criticism: it is to identify in a text the structure of roles, relationships and values which are 'distinctly ideological'. The same values will be found in a variety of texts because they are those which shape the consciousness of the social class which produced the texts.

> We find embedded in Charlotte's work, for example, a constant struggle between two ambiguous, internally divided sets of values . . . the values of rationality, coolness, shrewd self-seeking, energetic individualism, radical protest and rebellion . . . and the habits of piety, submission, culture, tradition, conservatism . . . the elements of one may be displaced or 'inverted' into the other . . . a fictionally transformed version of the tensions and alliances between . . . the industrial bourgeoisie, and the landed gentry. (p. 4)

But novels are not simply representative of the situation of a particular class. Eagleton goes on to show how 'an individual life actively transforms the historical structures which determine it into a unique artistic product' (p. 7).

> These pervasive social conflicts were then peculiarly intensified by the sisters' personal situation. They were, to begin with, placed at a painfully ambiguous point in the social structure, as the daughters of a clergyman with the inferior status of 'perpetual curate' who had thrust his way up from poverty; they strove as a family to maintain reasonably 'genteel' standards in a traditionally rough-and-ready environment. They were, moreover, socially insecure *women* – members of a cruelly oppressed group whose victimised condition reflected a more widespread exploitation. And they were *educated* women, trapped in an almost intolerable deadlock between culture and economics – between imaginative aspiration and the cold truth of a society which could use them merely as 'higher' servants. They were *isolated* educated women, socially and geographically remote from a world with which they nonetheless maintained close intellectual touch, and so driven back on themselves in solitary emotional hungering . . .' And as if all this were not enough, they were forced to endure in their childhood an especially brutal form of ideological oppression – Calvinism. (p. 8)

Eagleton sees Charlotte Brontë's novels as 'myths' which try to fuse 'blunt bourgeois rationality and flamboyant Romanticism, brash initiative and genteel cultivation, passionate rebellion and cautious conformity' (p. 4). He defines their basic structure as a power-relationship between a woman and a man, one subservient to the other, in whom are blended the conflicting characteristics of the 'Romantic-radical' and 'autocratic conservative'. The tension in her novels between 'romance' and 'realism' is thus a metaphor for these conflicting and ambiguous ideologies:

> Romantic emotion, guiltily thrust back on itself, becomes a smothered protest against a society which by denying vision distorts it into

> billowing fantasy; and in the 'higher' figure it emerges as a vivaciously radical *panache*. But at the same time the full gush of that emotion is typically channelled into a heady celebration of the heroic, a lurid, slipshod exaltation of the patriotic, the traditionalist, the doggedly provincial. . . . 'Realism' contains an equal political ambivalence. It emerges on the one hand as a critical, clear-sighted refusal to be mystified by the regalia of rank and despotic power; and as such it incarnates a liberal-egalitarian ethic, progressive in its scorn of upper-class privilege and cant, intimately responsive to the solid, sober and suffering. But its most salient feature is bourgeois ambition, cloaked and unconfessed to varying degrees – an ambition which, while fiercely contesting the system which denies it full growth, inevitably takes that system as its cherished end. (p. 76)

The marriage in which the power-relationship in *Jane Eyre* ends is seen by Eagleton as a compromise on Jane's part. Rochester's physical dependence on her enables her to be at once subservient and powerful in her love. The fact that the novel ends with Rivers's words underlies, in Eagleton's view, the compromise which Jane, unlike her cousin, has made between the world and the spirit. Such an argument clearly contradicts the view that Jane's marriage is presented as an achievement, representing social and sexual equality.

This reading of the novel's ending is related to Jane's conception of equality throughout the novel. Although in many ways she appears to challenge the class structure, insisting on her spiritual equality with her 'master', her attitudes also implicitly endorse it. Eagleton demonstrates this very effectively in discussing Jane's attitude towards her pupils in Morton, and her haste to make clear to Hannah, the Rivers's servant, that however poor she appears, she is nevertheless a *lady*. As he puts it, 'Far from offering a radically alternative ethic, spiritual equality is what actually smooths your progress through the class-system' (p. 29). The hierarchy of moral worth which we discussed in Chapter 6 of this *Guide* (p. 65) seems therefore to represent a degree of complicity with the social hierarchy, rather than to repudiate it.

> In the end, the outcast bourgeoise achieves more than a humble place at the fireside: she also gains independence *vis-à-vis* the upper class, and the right to engage in the process of taming it. The wordly Rochester has already been purified by fire; it is now for Jane to rehumanise him. By the device of an ending, bourgeois initiative and genteel settlement, sober rationality and Romantic passion, spiritual equality and social distinction, the actively affirmative and the patiently deferential self, can be merged into mythical unity. (p. 32)

You can consider for yourself how far Charlotte Brontë is imprisoned by the attitudes of her class by returning to the concept of the 'natural' which I asked you to consider earlier in this chapter.

You will, I am sure, already have concluded that the novel implies Nature and the natural are benign – no-one is presented as 'naturally' vicious. But does the term have any social implications? Consider, for instance, Jane's pronouncement that, once received into the Rivers household, she 'dared to put off the mendicant – to resume [her] *natural* manner and character' (Ch. 28, p. 342).

DISCUSSION

The implications of this phrase to me are that she re-asserts her social status. In asserting that she is not by *nature* a beggar, only by force of circumstance, she surely implies that there are those who *are* beggars 'by nature'? By this she presumably means 'by birth', since she appears unprepared to accept any identity between herself and any 'normal' beggar, who might equally be seen as the victim of circumstance. Jane implies, moreover, that her social position is 'natural' to her, part of the 'real' Jane Eyre. She is, of course, maintaining a careful distinction between social and financial status, but this serves less to undermine the idea of class distinctions than to reinforce them, since they are given the 'natural' seal of approval. Similarly, when Rochester says, 'nature, at least, has stamped her patent of nobility on this brow' (Ch. 24, p. 261), he appears to assert that Jane's 'naturally' lady-like behaviour and appearance over-ride her dependent and impoverished situation. Yet this apparent repudiation of class distinctions turns out, in the light of the novel's ending, to be simply prophetic of Jane's re-instatement as gentry on receiving her uncle's inheritance. Her ladylike 'nature' exists not in spite of her humble social position, but as evidence of her true position by birth – proof that 'blood will out'.

Not all uses of the word 'natural' have these obvious class associations, but these examples indicate, I would suggest, the need for the reader to be constantly alert to the possible prejudices such apparently innocent terms represent.

Psycho-biographical Criticism

Finally, I want to consider briefly an example of psycho-biographical criticism. Such criticism locates the stimulus for the novel in Charlotte

Brontë's individual history – biographical and psychological – and interprets the novel in terms of that history, often as a response to some early psychological need or suffering. The most interesting recent studies go beyond the cruder 'autobiographical' readings which try to identify people, places and experiences in the novel with those in the life, but I myself have certain reservations about them. In the first place, they usually appear to rest on elaborate hypotheses about the author's inner life, and secondly they run the risk of ignoring the fact that the novel is a fictional construction.

Nevertheless, books such as Helene Moglen's *Charlotte Brontë: The Self Conceived* produce perceptive and thought-provoking readings: we have already considered what she has to say about the novel as a 'feminist myth'. What is distinctive about her approach is that she also interprets the novel in 'psychosexual terms', emphasizing the conflict in Charlotte Brontë between regressive sexual fantasy and the desire to assert the autonomous self. Moglen describes Brontë's art as a means of 'exploring and expressing aspects of her feeling for Branwell which she could not consciously accept'.[12] She had collaborated with her brother on the early Angrian tales, and appeared in these to collude with the male domination of the female characters. The later tales which she wrote independently, however, show her growing resistance to the appeal of that domination: they represent 'exercises in confrontation' in which she attempted to free herself from her relationship with Branwell. Branwell's physical and mental disintegration was, therefore, both essential to her self-discovery, and the cause of intense guilt. After the death of her brother and sisters, this guilt was intensified as the guilt of the survivor, and compounded with the masochistic submission that characterised her feelings for both brother and father.

You can consider for yourself whether Charlotte Brontë's presentation of Jane indicates a strong element of masochism, particularly in her relationship with men. Moglen suggests, for instance, that even the appeal of St John Rivers depends on the sado-masochistic element of sexuality, which underlies the attraction of power. But I would like to point out that such a reading does not necessarily depend on approaching the novel through the biography. Here is what Peter Coveney has to say about Jane's early experiences:

> There is a disturbing relish about the account of the physical and mental tortures she endures. It is as if she enjoys, masochistically, the experiences of her persecution. She seems almost to provoke her self-torment. There is no end to the spiral of deprivation, and its continuously intensifying craving for love. Every twist of the knife

> intensifies the expectation of gratification. Everything is carefully prepared for the extended sado-masochistic relation between Jane and Rochester which lies, of course, at the heart of the novel.[13]

When you come to read *The Self Conceived*, as I hope you will, you will have to decide not only whether you find such a reading of Jane's character convincing, but whether the location of the source of that characterization in Charlotte Brontë's biography makes it any more convincing than it would be if substantiated solely in terms of the text.

8. Biography and Literary Background

The extraordinary talent of the Brontë family and their tragic early deaths have inevitably attracted a great deal of attention to their lives, from their readers and the general public. I intend, however, to give you only the briefest outline of Charlotte Brontë's life, stressing the literary rather than the private side. If you want to know more, the Further Reading list recommends a number of biographies. I should point out, however, that whatever the interest of such studies, I am dubious about their value in illuminating our understanding of the novels themselves. Leaving aside the considerable difficulties in determining the 'facts' of Charlotte Brontë's life, and in interpreting those facts, we have to decide on the relevance of the life to the work. Once we have traced the 'original' of Lowood in Cowan Bridge School, what do we do with this information? We can use it, of course, to defend the novelist against charges of exaggeration, but

The Clergy Daughter's School Cowan Bridge

it does not help us to understand the function of the school in terms of the novel. The danger, indeed, is of being so overcome by the sense that 'this really happened', that we fail to attend to the way that aspect of the author's 'life' is transmuted into 'work'.

Bearing that general caveat in mind, though, let us summarize the main biographical facts. Charlotte Brontë was born in 1816, the third child of Patrick Brontë, a native of County Down in Ireland, and Maria Branwell, a Cornishwoman, who, together with their two elder daughters, Maria and Elizabeth, then lived in the parish of Bradford, where the Reverend Brontë, a clergyman of the Established Church, held the living of Thornton in the West Riding of Yorkshire. In 1817 her brother Branwell was born, followed by Emily Jane in 1818, and Anne in 1820. That same year the family moved to the parsonage at Haworth, also in the West Riding, and there Mrs Brontë died in 1821. Miss Elizabeth Branwell, Maria's sister, left Cornwall to look after the family in her sister's absence and remained with them till her death in 1842. In 1824 the four eldest girls were sent to Cowan Bridge in Lancashire, a recently-opened school for the daughters of poor clergymen. There, during an outbreak of 'fever' – possibly typhoid – in 1825, Maria and Elizabeth became ill and were sent home to die. Shortly thereafter Charlotte and Emily were also sent home, where they remained for the next six years.

At home with Anne and Branwell, Charlotte and Emily found increasing pleasure in writing. In 1826, Mr Brontë bought Branwell a box of toy soldiers, around which the children constructed not only numerous plays, but the more significant fantasy worlds of Angria, the invention of Charlotte and Branwell, and Gondal, the province of Anne and Emily. In 1831 Charlotte was sent to Miss Wooler's school at Roe Head, twenty miles from Haworth, for a year; there she met her two lifelong friends, Ellen Nussey and Mary Taylor. Over the following ten years Charlotte attempted to make a career out of teaching, both at Miss Wooler's school and as a governess. The unsatisfactoriness of this socially ambiguous position made her determined that she and Emily should open a school of their own. Consequently, in 1842 they went to the Pensionnat Héger in Brussels to obtain the essential qualification in French. Many believe that Charlotte there fell in love with Constantin Héger, the principal's husband, who taught in the school. After another spell at the school as a governess in 1843, she returned home to stay in 1844.

In 1845 Charlotte found a manuscript of Emily's verse, and persuaded her and Anne to join herself in publishing, at their own expense, a selection of poetry under the pseudonyms, Currer, Ellis and Acton Bell. Charlotte explained this choice of names in her

Preface to the 1850 edition of *Wuthering Heights* and *Agnes Grey*: the sisters, in particular Emily, felt they needed pseudonyms as protection against personal publicity. Not wishing to be so dishonest as to pretend to be men, they adopted ambiguous Christian names in order to avoid the kind of prejudiced reception they felt most women writers received. The following year, after the publication of the poems, the Brontës offered for publication three 'tales' – *The Professor*, by Charlotte, *Wuthering Heights* by Emily, and *Agnes Grey* by Anne. Although her sisters' novels were accepted, for publication in 1847, *The Professor*, Charlotte's first novel, met with the fate she later described to G. H. Lewes:

> You warn me to beware of melodrama, and you exhort me to adhere to the real. When I first began to write, so impressed was I with the truth of the principles you advocate, that I determined to take Nature and Truth as my sole guides, and to follow in their very footprints; I restrained imagination, eschewed romance, repressed excitement; over-bright colouring, too, I avoided, and sought to produce something which should be soft, grave, and true.
>
> My work (a tale in one volume) being completed, I offered it to a publisher. He said it was original, faithful to nature, but he did not feel warranted in accepting it; such a work would not sell. I tried six publishers in succession; they all told me it was deficient in 'startling incident' and 'thrilling excitement,' that it would never suit the circulating libraries, and, as it was on those libraries the success of works of fiction mainly depended, they could not undertake to publish what would be overlooked there.[1]

In 1846, however, while in Manchester with her father, who was undergoing an eye operation, Charlotte had begun *Jane Eyre*. Following *The Professor*'s failure, therefore, she sent a new manuscript to Smith, Elder and Co., who published it in October 1847 as *Jane Eyre*. Such was the novel's success that a second edition was required by the end of the year, and a third by the spring of 1848.

Following the publication and success of *Jane Eyre*, there was widespread speculation among readers and reviewers as to the sex and identity of Currer Bell. Although many recognized that the author was a woman, there was a suspicion that Ellis, Acton and Currer Bell might be one and the same person, since 'the Bells' had appeared together as authors of the *Poems*. Thomas Newby, the publisher of *Wuthering Heights* and *Agnes Grey*, encouraged this rumour by wording his advertisements for these novels in such a way as to imply that they, too, were the work of Smith's famous new novelist. When George Smith, Charlotte's publisher, wished to be able to contradict this rumour, Charlotte and Anne decided to reassure him with living proof of their separate identities – Emily, as always, refused to leave Haworth unless it was unavoidable. Accordingly, the two sisters went to London to see George Smith in July, 1848.

More success followed later that year with the publication of Anne's second novel, *The Tenant of Wildfell Hall*, but in September Branwell died of consumption, followed within months by Emily and Anne. Charlotte spent the following five years alone at Haworth with her father and his curate, Arthur Bell Nicholls, apart from annual visits to London where she made a number of literary friends, including Elizabeth Gaskell, whom she had first met at Lake Windermere, in August 1850. Her next novel, *Shirley*, was published in 1849 and generally well-received, as was *Villette*, published in 1853. In 1854, after much persistence on Mr Nicholls's part, and much opposition on her father's, Charlotte married Arthur Nicholls, but died less than a year later of consumption, probably complicated by her pregnancy.

As already indicated, *Jane Eyre* was an immediate and dramatic success, interest in the novel being intensified by the mystery surrounding the sex and identity of its author. It was, nevertheless, frequently condemned by critics for its 'coarseness', and the 'indecorous' treatment of love. One such review, hostile on moral grounds, appeared in *The Quarterly Review* in 1848: Elizabeth Rigby accused the author of committing, in her portrayal of Rochester, 'that highest moral offence a novel writer can commit, that of making an unworthy character interesting in the eyes of the reader'.[2] The *Christian Remembrancer* denounced the novel for being anti-Christian and revolutionary: 'Every page burns with moral Jacobinism. "Unjust, unjust", is the burden of every reflection upon the things and powers that be.'[3] Another focus for attack was the implausibility of the plot, particularly the Gothic elements in the Thornfield section.

Most critics, however, praised the novel for creating a new and heightened reality, perceiving the originality with which Charlotte Brontë had used the Gothic conventions. 'Power' is a term often used to describe a sense of reality strong enough to outweigh the improbabilities. G. H. Lewes saw 'deep, significant reality' in the novel, in spite of 'too much melodrama and improbability'.[4] Most reviews paid tribute to the novel's truthful observation of everyday reality heightened by intense feeling, and later critics continued to admire this aspect of the work. Here is one example:

> How often in the early scenes of childhood or school-life does one instinctively expect the conventional solution, the conventional

> softening, the conventional prettiness or quaintness. . . . And it never comes. Hammer-like, the blows of a passionate realism descend. Jane Eyre, the little helpless child, is never comforted; Mrs Reed, the cruel aunt, is never sorry for her cruelties; Bessie, the kind nurse, is not *very* kind.[5]

Following Charlotte's death, and the publication of Mrs Gaskell's biography, which aimed to 'make the world . . . honour the woman as much as they have admired the writer'[6], the novelist was increasingly seen as a moralist, rather than a rebel. Critics refuted earlier charges of 'coarseness' by emphasizing the ultimately *moral* purpose of a novel like *Jane Eyre*. Nevertheless, late Victorian critics continued to find the novel rather 'revolutionary' in its sentiments. This debate about the novelist's 'respectability' continued, and in the twentieth century ironically led to a lowering of Charlotte's reputation in relation to Emily's. Charlotte's novels came to be seen as purveying simple moral certainties, whereas her sister's novel was appreciated for its more complex and original treatment of moral issues.[7] In recent years, the balance has shifted again, more attention now being paid to Charlotte's novels as texts, rather than as sources for biographical conjecture.[8]

In conclusion, I would like to suggest that if you want to study the novel's relationship to the literary tradition there are two lines of approach worth following. The first is that adopted by Kathleen Tillotson in her book, *Novels of the 1840s*. Professor Tillotson argues that the novels written in this period share certain characteristics which initiated new trends. In contrast to earlier novels of fashionable society, these extended the novel's social range, enlightening their middle-class readers. There was a new emphasis on moral and religious controversy, the religious emphasis encouraging the growing tendency to introspection in the novel. Professor Tillotson cites as influential factors not only the prevailing social and political situation, but writers like Scott and Carlyle, who awakened 'the poetic, prophetic and visionary possibilities of the novel'.[9] She sees *Jane Eyre* itself as the novel least related to its time of those she discusses, believing that its emphasis on the solitary inner life aligns it more closely with the poetry of the period. She goes on:

> Nevertheless it belongs to the eighteen-forties. Its flying start – extraordinary for the first publication of an unknown author – would have been inconceivable ten years earlier or later: it would have been too 'low' in social level for 1837, too outspoken for 1857. In 1847 it had apparently not more novelty than was welcome; the 'new' was hooked not only to the 'natural', but to what was already becoming familiar in novels. A survey of reviews and private contemporary references shows that the average intelligent novel-reader . . . acclaimed

> *Jane Eyre* as a work of genius; there is no sign that he was antagonized by the novelties of setting and social level; they were new but not startlingly so.[10]

Charlotte Brontë's own disclaimer – 'I cannot write books handling the topics of the day; it is of no use trying'[11] – appears to substantiate Professor Tillotson's reservations about the novel's relationship to its period. However I would suggest that the novel is deeply engaged with such 'topics of the day' as the position of women, particularly of governesses, education and religious orthodoxies, while its Yorkshire setting, still relatively unknown territory in the literary world, extends the novel's social and literary range in precisely the same way as other 'novels of the 1840s'.

Raymond Williams takes this question of the novel's relationship with the 1840s further, looking for more than a surface concern with the prevailing social and political issues. In examining the 'structure of feeling' which links the novels of both Charlotte and Emily Brontë with their time, he too brings out their links with the Romantic poets:

> The world we need to remember if we are to see these connections of the 1840s is the world of Blake: a world of desire and hunger, of rebellion and of pallid convention: the terms of desire and fulfilment and the terms of oppression and deprivation profoundly connected in a single dimension of experience. . . . I think we need to start from the feeling, the central feeling, that an intensity of desire is as much a response, a deciding response, to the human crisis of that time as the more obviously recognizable political radicalism. Indeed, to give that kind of value to human longing and need, to that absolute emphasis on commitment to another, the absolute love of the being of another, is to clash as sharply with the emerging system, the emerging priorities, as in any assault on material poverty.[12]

The originality of the sisters, Professor Williams suggests, lies in their reshaping of the novel to give direct expression to this intensity of feeling.

Furthermore, this intensity of feeling marks a break with a tradition that was not only familiar, but male. In bringing out this aspect of the novel, Raymond Williams brings us to the second line of approach I want to consider. Inga-Stina Ewbank relates the novel to a specifically female tradition. She traces three strands in women's fiction: romance, often in a Gothic or historical context, the fashionable novel of high life, and the didactic novel, usually in a middle-class setting.[13] The didacticism of the last group was often presented as the only possible justification for women writing at all, and was in the 1840s directed specifically into those areas of social concern mentioned by Kathleen Tillotson. While Professor Ewbank indicates the relationship *Jane Eyre* bears to this tradition of women's writing, often overlooked in more orthodox studies of 'the literary tradition', she too shows how far Charlotte Brontë breaks with tradition: her novels were often condemned as 'unwomanly' precisely because of that awareness of passion mentioned above.

Notes

Chapter One: Who is Jane Eyre? (Pages 1–13)

1 'The Place of Love in *Jane Eyre* and *Wuthering Heights*', in *The Brontës: A Collection of Critical Essays*, edited by Ian Gregor (Twentieth Century Views), Prentice-Hall, 1970, pp. 80–81. All further references to this collection will be abbreviated to *Twentieth Century Views*.
2 *My Heart Leaps Up*, 1807. Margaret Smith discusses Charlotte Brontë's affinity with Wordsworth in her Introduction to the World's Classics edition of *Jane Eyre* (p. ix).
3 *The Image of Childhood: the Individual and Society: a Study of the Theme in English Literature*, Penguin, 1967, pp. 31–2.
4 *Ibid.*, p. 92.
5 See Wayne C. Booth, *The Rhetoric of Fiction*, University of Chicago, 1961, pp. 3–20, for a fuller discussion of these terms.
6 See Marvin Mudrick, *Jane Austen: Irony as Defense and Discovery*, Princeton University Press, 1952.
7 Karen Chase, *Eros and Psyche: The Representation of Personality in Charlotte Brontë, Charles Dickens, George Eliot*, New York, Methuen, 1984, pp. 50–51.
8 *Ibid.*, p. 51.
9 Karl Kroeber, *Styles in Fictional Structure: The Art of Jane Austen, Charlotte Brontë, George Eliot*, Princeton University Press, 1971, p. 46.
10 For a more complex view of this issue, see Tony Tanner, 'Passion, narrative and identity in *Wuthering Heights* and *Jane Eyre*', in *Teaching the Text*, edited by Susanne Kappeler and Norman Bryson, Routledge and Kegan Paul, 1983, pp. 109–125. Tanner argues that Jane can be seen as *constructing* herself through the act of narration. See Chapter 7 for some discussion of this point.

Chapter Two: Characterization (Pages 14–25)

1 See Chapter 4 of this *Guide* for a fuller discussion of realism.
2 *Structuralist Poetics: Structuralism, Linguistics and the Study of Literature*, Routledge and Kegan Paul, 1975, p. 225. This book is one of the most useful introductions to structuralist criticism, particularly as it relates to realist fiction.

3 *S/Z*, translated by Richard Miller, Hill and Wang, 1974, pp. 67 and 191. Originally published in French as *S/Z*, Editions du Seuil, 1970.
4 *Op. cit.*, p. 62.
5 See, for example, Wolfgang Iser, *The Act of Reading: A Theory of Aesthetic Response*, Routledge and Kegan Paul, 1978.
6 The pseudo-science of phrenology was made popular in the nineteenth century by George Coombe's *Elements of Phrenology* (1828). The 'science' developed from the theory that each individual's mental powers consisted of separate faculties, each located in a distinct region of the surface of the brain. Study of the skull's shape would, therefore, indicate the relative development of each faculty. Charlotte Brontë visited a fashionable phrenologist in London, in 1851 (see Elizabeth Gaskell, *The Life of Charlotte Brontë* (1857), ed. by Alan Shelston, Penguin English Library, 1975, p. 613).
7 See Michael Wheeler, *The Art of Allusion in Victorian Fiction*, Macmillan, 1979.
8 Robert Martin, *The Accents of Persuasion: Charlotte Brontë's Novels*, Faber, 1966, p. 64.
9 You can pursue this approach by reading Karen Chase, '*Jane Eyre*'s Interior Design', *op. cit.*, pp. 47–65.
10 Andrew D. Hook, 'Charlotte Brontë, the Imagination, and *Villette*', *Twentieth Century Views*, p. 149.

Chapter Three: Language (Pages 25–38)

1 *The Language of Fiction: Essays in Criticism and Verbal Analysis of the English Novel*, Routledge and Kegan Paul, 1966, pp. 114–143.
2 'Objective correlative' is a term coined by T. S. Eliot for concrete objects or situations used in a literary work to arouse a specific emotion required by the author. See Eliot's essay on *Hamlet* (1919), reprinted in *Selected Essays* (3rd edition), Faber and Faber, 1953, pp. 141–6.
3 For an analysis of spatial imagery in the novel, see Karen Chase, *op. cit.*, pp. 61–2.
4 *Op. cit.*, p. 80.
5 See p. 57 for further discussion of this issue.
6 See Tanner, *op. cit.*, p. 116.
7 For a fuller discussion of transformational grammar, and those aspects of linguistics most relevant to students of literature, see Roger Fowler, *Linguistics and the Novel*, Methuen, 1977.
8 See Margot Peters, *Charlotte Brontë: Style in the Novel*, University of Wisconsin Press, 1973, pp. 44–45.
9 Ibid., p. 41.
10 Fowler, *op. cit.*, p. 103.
11 *Ibid.*, p. 106.

Chapter Four: Realism or Romance? (Pages 39–52)

1 See David Lodge, '*Middlemarch* and the Idea of the Classic Realist Text', in *The Nineteenth-Century Novel: Critical Essays and Documents* (revised edition), ed. by Arnold Kettle, Open University

Press, 1981, pp. 218–38. For a more comprehensive discussion of 'realism' and 'romance', consult the following: Harry Levin, 'Romance and Realism', *The Gates of Horn: A Study of Five French Realists*, New York, Oxford University Press, 1963, pp. 24–83; Kenneth Graham, 'The Question of Realism', *English Criticism of the Novel 1865–1900*, Clarendon Press, 1965, pp. 19–70; Raymond Williams, 'Realism and the Contemporary Novel', *The Long Revolution*, Penguin Books, 1965, pp. 300–316; Gillian Beer, *The Romance*, (Critical Idiom), Methuen, 1970.

2 See Ian Watt, 'Realism and the Novel Form', *The Rise of the Novel*, Penguin Books, 1972, pp. 9–37.

3 Quoted in Gaskell, *op. cit.*, p. 338.

4 'Charlotte Brontë's "New" Gothic in *Jane Eyre* and *Villette*' (1958), reprinted in *Charlotte Brontë: 'Jane Eyre' and 'Villette': A Casebook*, edited by Miriam Allott, Macmillan, 1973, pp. 195–204 (hereafter referred to as *Casebook*).

5 *Legends of Angria: Compiled from the Early Writings of Charlotte Brontë by Fannie E. Ratchford*, ed. by W. C. DeVane, Kennikat Press, 1973, p. 316.

6 See, for example, Leslie Stephen, *Casebook*, p. 151.

7 *Christian Remembrancer*, 1848, *Casebook*, p. 59.

8 See Gaskell, *op. cit.*, p. 151.

9 Stephen, *Casebook*, p. 151.

10 Obituary article, quoted in Gaskell, *op. cit.*, p 308.

11 *Casebook*, p. 61.

12 *Op. cit.*, p. 85.

13 *Op. cit.*, p. 96.

14 'The Brontës: A Centennial Observance' (1947), re-printed in *Twentieth Century Views*, pp. 19–33. See Chapter 6, pp. 73–5 of this *Guide* for further discussion of Lawrence's view of *Jane Eyre*.

15 *The Cover of the Mask: The Autobiographers in Charlotte Brontë's Fiction*, University of Victoria, 1982, p. 58.

16 For discussion of this concept, see Eva Figes, *Patriarchal Attitudes: Women in Society*, Panther Books, 1972.

17 *Charlotte Brontë: The Self Conceived*, Norton, 1976, p. 30.

18 Op. cit., p. 59.

Chapter Five: Structure and Theme (Pages 52–63)

1 You can pursue this argument by reading Jonathan Culler's critique of Roman Jakobson, the Russian formalist (*op. cit.*, pp. 56–65), which suggests that, because we *expect* structures to have meaning, they cannot, in the end, be 'objective'.

2 *Novels of the Eighteen-Forties*, Oxford University Press, 1954, pp. 286–7. 'Glass Town' and 'Verdopolis' are the names of towns in Charlotte Brontë's fictional world of Angria.

3 *Op. cit.*, pp. 80–85.

4 See *S/Z*, p. 55, and the section on 'Post-structuralism' in Chapter 7 of this *Guide* (pp. 82–5). The distinction between 'paradigmatic' and 'syntagmatic' was developed by the Swiss linguist, Ferdinand de

Saussure. See Robert Scholes, *Structuralism in Literature: An Introduction*, Yale University Press, 1974, pp. 13–22.
5 R. B. Martin, *op. cit.*, p. 81.
6 e.g. Margot Peters, who bases her reading of the novel on what she sees as its pervasive legal language (*op. cit.*, pp. 146–53).

Chapter Six: The Morality of the Novel (Pages 63–76)

1 See, however, Terry Eagleton's view, summarized in the section on Marxist criticism in Chapter 7 (pp. 87–90), that this hierarchy of moral worth sustains, rather than challenges, the class structure.
2 For a variety of interpretations of this incident, see the following: Sandra Gilbert and Susan Gubar, *'The Madwoman in the Attic': The Woman Writer and the Nineteenth-Century Imagination*, Yale University Press, 1979, p. 367; Kinkead-Weekes, *op. cit.*, p. 84; Martin, *op. cit.* p. 96; Barry Qualls, *The Secular Pilgrims of Victorian Fiction: The Novel as Book of Life*, Cambridge University Press, 1982, pp. 67–9.
3 *The Brontës and their Background: Romance and Reality*, Macmillan, 1973.
4 Qualls, *op. cit.*, p. 13. Qualls's chapter on Charlotte Brontë, 'The terrible beauty of Charlotte Brontë's "Natural Supernaturalism"', pp. 43–84, presents a difficult argument, but one that is well worth reading.
5 See e.g. Lodge, *op. cit.*, p. 135.
6 *Op. cit.*, p. 68.
7 *Op. cit.*, pp. 60–61.
8 See *S/Z*, pp. 97–8 and pp. 205–6; and p. 84 of this *Guide*.
9 'Pornography and Obscenity', *Phoenix: The Posthumous Papers of D. H. Lawrence*, ed. by Edward D. MacDonald, Heinemann, 1936, pp. 174–7.
10 I have drawn in this paragraph on the ideas of Jacques Lacan, a French psychoanalyst, whose theories relate Freudian psychology to the human subject's relationship to language, and on those of Louis Althusser, a French Marxist philosopher, who uses Lacan's theory to explain the process by which human subjects submit themselves to ideology. For an introduction to these very complex ideas, see Terry Eagleton, *Literary Theory: An Introduction*, Basil Blackwell, 1983, pp. 163–174; and *Modern Literary Theory: A Comparative Introduction*, ed. by Ann Jefferson and David Robey, Batsford, 1982, pp. 119–132.
11 For a similar reading, although expressed in different terms, see Annette Tromly's interpretation, discussed in Chapter 7, 'Recent Critical Approaches'.

Chapter Seven: Recent Critical Approaches (Pages 76–92)

1 See Further Reading.
2 *Narrative Discourse: An Essay in Method*, Oxford University Press, 1980.
3 *Ibid.*, p. 102.

4 See Note (15) to Chapter 4. All page references to this text will follow the relevant quotation.
5 *Op. cit.*, pp. 115–118.
6 All page references to this text follow the relevant quotation.
7 See Terry Eagleton, *Literary Theory: An Introduction*, Basil Blackwell, 1983, pp. 135–6. Much of the argument contained in this section of the chapter is indebted to Eagleton's analysis.
8 For a fuller account of this subject, see Jonathan Culler, *On Deconstruction: Theory and Criticism after Structuralism*, Routledge and Kegan Paul, 1983.
9 *Op. cit.*, p. xi. All page references to this text follow the relevant quotation.
10 For a different kind of 'deconstruction', an imaginative re-construction of Bertha's point of view, read Jean Rhys's novel, *Wide Sargasso Sea*, Penguin, 1968.
11 *Myths of Power: A Marxist Study of the Brontës*, Macmillan, 1975. All page references to this text follow the relevant quotation.
12 Moglen, *op. cit.* All page references to this text follow the relevant quotation.
13 *Op. cit.*, p. 107.

Chapter Eight: Biography and Literary Background (Pages 92–98)

1 Quoted in Gaskell, *op. cit.*, p. 329.
2 Quoted in *Casebook*, p. 68.
3 *Ibid.*, p. 58.
4 *Ibid.*, pp. 52–4.
5 Mary Ward, Introduction to Haworth edition of *Jane Eyre* (1898), quoted in *The Brontë's: The Critical Heritage*, edited by Miriam Allott, Routledge and Kegan Paul, 1974, p. 449.
6 Gaskell, *op. cit.*, p. 14.
7 See e.g. Lord David Cecil's essays in *Early Victorian Novelists*, 1934. The major part of his essay on Charlotte is reprinted in *Casebook*, pp. 167–74.
8 Wendy Craik, *The Brontë Novels*, Methuen, 1968, was one of the first and most helpful critical works to approach the novels in this way.
9 *Op. cit.*, p. 154.
10 *Ibid.*, pp. 258–9.
11 Letter to George Smith, her publisher, 1852, quoted in Gaskell, *op. cit.*, p. 483.
12 *The English Novel from Dickens to Lawrence*, Paladin, 1974, pp. 50–51.
13 *Their Proper Sphere: The Brontës as Female Novelists*, Edward Arnold, 1966.

Suggestions for Further Reading

As well as those books and articles already referred to in the text, you will find the following selection helpful.

Biographical

Mrs Gaskell's biography of Charlotte Brontë (see Notes) was constrained by a number of factors: many of the people mentioned were still alive, and hostile to the views expressed in the first edition; she did not have access to all Charlotte Brontë's letters to Ellen Nussey; above all, she was intent on portraying the 'good' Charlotte as a corrective to the earlier popular view of the anti-Christian radical. Nevertheless, this first biography remains fascinating reading.

For a more up-to-date view, Margaret Lane, *The Brontë Story: A Reconsideration of Mrs Gaskell's Life of Charlotte Brontë*, Heinemann, 1953, is an edited version of the Gaskell original, adding material, particularly that relating to M. Héger, which Mrs Gaskell omitted. The most comprehensive account remains Winifred Gérin, *Charlotte Brontë: The Evolution of Genius*, Clarendon Press, 1967, but Phyllis Bentley, *The Brontës and their World*, Thames and Hudson, 1968, provides a brief and very readable introduction to the subject.

Critical studies

For a comprehensive anthology of reviews and criticism, contemporary and modern, consult *The Brontës: The Critical Heritage*, edited by Miriam Allott, Routledge and Kegan Paul, 1974. Some of the most interesting material relating to Charlotte Brontë is, however, also contained in the Macmillan Casebook, *Charlotte Brontë: 'Jane Eyre' and 'Villette'*, edited by Miriam Allott, 1973. This very useful source-book contains several of the essays referred to in this *Guide* (see Notes), as does another good collection in the Twentieth Century Views series, *The Brontës: A Collection of Critical Essays*, edited by Ian Gregor, Prentice-Hall, 1970.

Recent critical theory

One of the best introductions to structuralist literary theory is Robert Scholes, *Structuralism in Literature: An Introduction*, Yale University Press, 1974. After this, try *Structuralism and Since: From Lévi-Strauss to Derrida*, edited by John Sturrock, Oxford University Press, 1979, an anthology of structuralist and post-structuralist writing on anthropology, as well as other disciplines more closely related to literary criticism. Also helpful is Terence Hawkes, *Structuralism and Semiotics*, Methuen, 1977.

Tony Bennett, *Formalism and Marxism*, Methuen, 1979, provides an excellent introduction to the Russian formalists, including Jakobson, and to Marxist criticism, which you could follow up with Terry Eagleton, *Marxism and Literary Criticism*, Methuen, 1976.

For an anthology of 'reception theory', criticism dealing with the role of the reader in the text, read *Reader-Response Criticism*, edited by Jane P. Tompkins, Baltimore, 1980.

Finally, for a broad overall view, consult the following: Terry Eagleton, *Literary Theory: An Introduction*, Blackwell, 1983; *Modern Literary Theory: A Comparative Introduction*, edited by Ann Jefferson and David Robey, Batsford, 1982.

Index